lemongrass & limes

thai flavors with Naam Pruitt

lemongrass & limes
Thai Flavors with Naam Pruitt

Published by Niramol Pruitt
© 2006 by
Niramol Pruitt
P.O. Box 1243
Independence, Kansas 67301
620-331-4055

Food Photography © by Steve Lalich
Food Styling by Julee Rauch

Library of Congress Control Number: 2005908824
ISBN: 0-9771527-0-7

Edited, Designed, and Manufactured by
Favorite Recipes® Press
an imprint of

FRP

P.O. Box 305142
Nashville, Tennessee 37230
800-358-0560

Art Director: Steve Newman
Book Design: Sheri Ferguson
Project Editor: Anna Watson

Printed in China
First Printing 2006
10,000 copies

dedication

I dedicate this book to two very special Proverbs 31 women in
my life. Mom, thank you for all the delicious and beautiful food you lovingly
prepared for us without complaining or stressing out and for the example
you set as a wife and mother. You always have a smile on your face.
I am most blessed to have a role model like you.

Myrt, without your constant encouragement I never would have gotten
started on this book. Thank you for having faith in me. You are the epitome
of how a boss should be. Your kind and loving example has impacted my
life tremendously. I am exceedingly thankful to have you in my life.

I love both of you so much.

table of contents

Acknowledgments   6

Preface   7

New Converts   10

Traditional Dinner   20

Esaan Style for Everyone   28

Satisfying Seafood   36

Thai Lunch Box   44

Vegetarians Only   52

Curry in a Hurry   60

Noodles Noodles   68

Refreshingly Low-Fat   74

Everyday Home Cooking   80

Street Snacks   90

More Desserts, Please!   98

Garnishing Ideas & Techniques   108

Glossary of Ingredients   112

Index   120

Order Information   125

 symbolizes a dish that can be made in 30 minutes or less.

acknowledgments

To Dave Kempf, Vice President of FRP, thank you for taking me seriously. I'd like to thank Bill Branch, my publishing consultant at FRP, who was continuously encouraging and helpful throughout this project. You are so pleasant and fun to work with. Thank you to Anna Watson and her editing team, for working so hard on this book. Anna, I truly appreciate your enthusiasm and love for my book. You are wonderful to work with. To everyone at FRP, thank you so much for sharing your experience with me. Thank you to all my sponsors. Thank you, Kate Brooks, for seeing my potential and introducing me to Thai Kitchen. To my dear friend Paul Kritz, thanks for your legal advice. To my banker friend Brad Oakes, thanks for your financial advice.

I had some wonderful assistants. My young friends Sammie Baumgartner and Jenni Jabben were a great help in preparing for the photo shoot. Carey Stalford was a joy to work with and did an outstanding job in easing my load during the photo shoot. She was a great assistant. Also many thanks to the wonderful businesses in Independence, Kansas, that helped with the photo shoot: Twigs, The Health Alternative, and the Garden Station (especially Shelly Shrader).

This book wouldn't be beautiful if it weren't for Lalich Photography. Steve, you sure know how to capture the essence of food through a lens. Not only are you wonderful at what you do, you are so much fun to work with. To Julee Rauch, my food stylist, your artful eyes turn ordinary items into extraordinary setups. I truly love working with you guys. I look forward to future projects with you. You are my new friends.

And most importantly, my family. Bennett and Anna, you are my pride and joy. You bring much laughter into my life. Your endless compliments on my food mean a lot to me. Thank you for being supportive and patient. I love you with all my heart. To my husband and soul mate, Dennis, without you this project wouldn't have come to life. Thank you for your faith in me, your support, and your daily encouragement. I appreciate so much your giving up your reading nights to type my recipes for me. For all the things you do for me, I cannot thank you enough. You are the love of my life.

preface

Thai food has always been in my blood. I was born in Prachuabkirikhan, the city located in the narrowest part of Thailand. It is a beautiful town along the sea, about four hours south of Bangkok. Fishing is a main part of the economy, so from an early age, I was blessed with fresh seafood. My father was raised by Thai Buddhist monks, and he served the Thai government as a spy in Burma. He also worked as a journalist and photographer for *Thai Rhat*, a national Thai newspaper. My mother comes from a large Thai family. Throughout my childhood, she took me to the fresh market and taught me how to find the best fruits, vegetables, and meat for the best prices. My mom is a fantastic cook. With her magical hands, everything she makes is outstanding. I learned how to master the subtle techniques and skills of Thai food by watching her cook every day for our family and for the many friends that stopped by. She is my role model.

As I was growing up, my life was like all the other Thai girls in school: studies, uniforms, and more studies. Then I had the opportunity to be an exchange student in Salibury, Maryland. It caused quite a stir at home, as I neglected to tell my dad I had submitted an application until after I was accepted. Reluctantly, he agreed to allow me to move across the ocean for one year, as he knew how much I loved to speak English. It would be the first of many trips to the United States. Soon after I returned to Thailand, I met my future husband. He liked me immediately, but I wasn't too sure about him. He was very interesting, a guy from Iowa who had spent part of his high school years in Malaysia and Thailand while his father worked on some engineering projects. Now he was back in Bangkok after a year in France. We met at church. He asked me to be his Thai tutor while he waited for the next term at language school to open. I was struck by how quickly he learned Thai. He told me later that he studied hard every night to impress me.

While Mom liked him right away, my dad was not happy with my decision to marry Dennis. He eventually accepted him after receiving the dowry (a set of nice leather living room furniture), but he wasn't happy until we had a son. I think it also helped that Dennis got a job. Now after two children and fifteen years of marriage, both my parents are quite happy with my husband (as am I). While I knew how to cook, I didn't realize how much I loved to cook until I got married. We began inviting friends over for Thai food once a week. Some were familiar with Thai food, while others needed an introduction.

Several years later, after many fun evenings in the dining room with friends, cooking my native food is still my favorite pastime. One evening, while I was preparing a Thai feast for my dear friend Myrt Davidson, she encouraged me to take the Thai flavors from the kitchen and place them in a book for our friends to enjoy. This work is for Thai people far from home and for Westerners who enjoy the exotic and unique flavors of Thai food. I hope you find my recipes fun and helpful, and that this book will allow you to share with your friends and family the wonderful tastes of Thailand.

It has been my aim to preserve for my children and others the traditional Thai cuisine handed down to me from my mother. The recipes you will discover in this book are genuine native dishes of Thailand. I live in the Midwest, and I know how difficult it can be to find some of the key Thai ingredients. I have included suggestions on how to adapt the recipes to your local grocery store.

I have organized most of the chapters into themes to ease your meal preparation. There are suggested menus for you to follow, but feel free to mix and match. Each dish can stand on its own, so you can pick any of the recipes for your family without having to do the entire menu. However, Thai food taps into a wide array of tastes, so not all dishes complement each other. I suggest you follow the suggested menus at first to better understand which flavors work together. With the exception of noodle dishes, all main courses are to be eaten with rice. There are a couple of chapters in the à la carte style so you can choose whatever sounds good to you.

To have a successful party, it's important not only to have food that tastes good, but also to have a sufficient amount of food. A general guideline is to prepare one dish per person, or one more dish than the number of people in your party. For example, if you have four people for supper, serve four or five different dishes. One interesting bit of information about the Thai style of dining is that Thais don't pass dishes around the table; we place the dishes at the center of the table and serve ourselves one serving spoonful at a time. I've adapted my style of dining by serving the food in courses, so as to encourage my friends to slowly enjoy the unique flavors of each dish. Don't be frustrated with the long list of ingredients in some recipes. After stocking your pantry with Thai supplies your second meal will be easier.

Throughout the book there are several recipes marked with a 🍍 . These dishes are "quick and easy," meaning that in less than thirty minutes you will have a tasty meal ready (including preparation and cooking time). I prepare these dishes frequently since my children are young and active in sports and other activities. I urge you to try them, too. You will find personal tips in all the recipes as if you were in my cooking class. I'll walk you through a detailed glossary of ingredients and I will recommend what brands to use. I'll also identify what substitutes to use in case you don't have access to an Asian grocery store.

You will notice that I don't include a lot of Thai desserts. For most of you, it is too difficult to find the right ingredients in the United States, even in an Asian grocery store. A genuine dessert from Thailand can be as simple as a tropical fruit platter. Instead, I have included some of my favorite tropical desserts, which I have created and served for many years—the perfect complement to Thai food.

My favorite thing about entertaining is making my guests feel special by making the food beautiful. You will learn several garnishing tips, such as how to create a tomato rose. You will be able to present your food with unique garnishing ideas. Some techniques are easy, while others require some practice.

I hope this book inspires you to get together with your family and friends to enjoy the most refreshing, full-flavored dishes in your own home. Have fun cooking!

Sawaddee kah,

Naam

new converts

Spring Rolls with Pork Filling
Pork Satay
Pad Thai
Coconut Ice Cream
Watermelon Smoothie

This first menu is the most popular with Westerners. When I invite guests for a Thai dinner and they have never tried Thai food before, this is the menu I use. While quite savory, it isn't too spicy, making it a nice introduction to Thai cuisine.

The menu will serve four adults with leftover spring rolls. Fry only as many spring rolls as you need, as they lose their crispiness when reheated. I encourage you to make the spring rolls in advance, without frying, and freeze them. Even the Pork Satay can be marinated and stored in the freezer. Just thaw out the pork the night before and skewer it in the morning.

Time-saving tips

One month before
Prepare the Spring Rolls and freeze.

One week before
Marinate the Pork Satay and freeze. Prepare the Simple Syrup for the smoothie.

3 days before
Prepare the Satay Sauce and refrigerate. Prepare the ice cream and freeze.

Morning of the dinner
Thaw out the Spring Rolls and Pork Satay. Prep all the ingredients for the Pad Thai. Cover and store the ingredients in separate containers in the refrigerator until ready to use. Cut up the vegetables for the Cucumber Relish. Cube and seed the watermelon.

If you love the fried egg rolls at Chinese restaurants, this is the dish for you. Instead of an all-vegetable filling, I pack them with ground pork. The spring rolls are lip-smacking good when served with sweet sauce. What makes this recipe so inviting is the fact that it's freezer-friendly.

Spring Rolls with Pork Filling

(bpaw-bpia-sai-moo)

1 small package glass noodles (one bundle)

2 tablespoons canola oil

2 garlic cloves, chopped

2 shallots, sliced

1 pound ground pork

1 teaspoon coriander

1 tablespoon sugar

3 tablespoons light soy sauce

1 tablespoon sweet soy sauce

1/4 cup chopped cilantro

2 large carrots, grated

1 (25-count) package frozen square spring roll wrappers, thawed

1 egg yolk, beaten

3 to 4 cups canola oil for deep frying

Makes 25 spring rolls

- Soak the glass noodles in water in a bowl for 15 minutes or until tender. Drain and coarsely chop the noodles.
- Heat the wok over medium-high heat until hot. Add 2 tablespoons oil, the garlic and shallots and cook until the garlic and shallots are golden brown, stirring constantly. Add the pork and stir-fry until the pork until is crumbly and opaque. Add the glass noodles, coriander, sugar, light soy sauce and sweet soy sauce. Cook until the noodles are translucent, stirring constantly. Stir in the cilantro and carrots. Remove from the heat and let cool completely.
- Place 1 spring roll wrapper on a smooth dry surface. Cover the remaining wrappers with damp paper towels. Rotate the wrapper 45 degrees, so it forms a diamond shape rather than a square. Place 2 tablespoons of the filling in the bottom half of the wrapper. Fold the bottom corner of the wrapper over the filling and roll 1/4 of the way up. Fold the 2 sides toward the center. Roll upward, leaving a 1-inch corner at the top. Brush a small amount of the egg yolk on the remaining wrapper and finish rolling. Repeat the process until all of the filling has been used. If there are any unused wrappers, they may be frozen for later use.
- Heat 3 to 4 cups of oil to 375 degrees in a large, heavy-bottomed deep skillet. Fry the spring rolls in small batches for 1 minute per side or until golden brown; drain on paper towels. For best results, let the oil reheat between batches.
- Serve the spring rolls with Spring Roll Sauce (page 13) for dipping. Eat the spring rolls with your fingers as an appetizer.

Note: Carrots are not a typical Thai vegetable, but I add them for their texture, flavor, and nutritional value. You may omit them if you like. Also, you may reuse the frying oil one more time; strain it and store in an airtight container.

Spring Roll Sauce

(naam-jim-bpaw-bpia)

1 cup water

4 cups dried salted plums

1¹/4 cups sugar

¹/2 teaspoon salt

2 tablespoons vinegar

1 tablespoon ground fresh red chili peppers

Makes 1 cup

- Place the water, dried salted plums, sugar, salt, vinegar and chili peppers in a large sauce pan. Bring to a boil over medium-high heat. Reduce the heat and simmer for 30 minutes, stirring occasionally.
- Strain the mixture and let cool. Pour into a jar with a tight-fitting lid and refrigerate for up to 6 months.

thai tidbit

There is a college for monkeys in Surathani, a southern province, to teach them how to retrieve coconuts from trees.

This is the most popular appetizer in Thailand, a very fun street food for both Thais and Westerners. It's common to find vendors on the sidewalk grilling the pork, especially near the marketplace. One day at my parents' house a group of American friends ate five kilograms (eleven pounds) of my mom's pork satay! This is traditionally a pork dish, though chicken makes an excellent substitute.

Pork Satay

(moo-satay)

หมูสะเต๊ะ

1 cup coconut milk (fresh or canned)

2 teaspoons turmeric powder, or
1 tablespoon fresh turmeric

1 teaspoon curry powder

1 tablespoon sugar

3 tablespoons light soy sauce

1 pound pork loin or butterfly pork, sliced
into long 1/4-inch thick strips

Wooden skewers

Satay Sauce (page 15)

Cucumber Relish (page 15)

Grilled bread

Serves 6 to 8 as an appetizer

- Whisk the coconut milk, turmeric powder, curry powder, sugar and soy sauce together in a bowl. Add the pork and marinate for 1 to 8 hours.
- Soak the skewers in water for 15 minutes to prevent burning. Remove the pork from the marinade, discarding the marinade. Thread the pork onto the skewers. Grill over hot coals or broil 3 inches from the heat source for 3 to 4 minutes per side.
- Serve with Satay Sauce, Cucumber Relish, and grilled bread or toast. Garnish with a tomato rose and cilantro.

Serving tip: No need for utensils with this dish; use the skewers to pick up the cucumbers.

thai tidbit

The largest diamond in the world belongs to the King of Thailand. He received it in honor of his fiftieth year of reign. It is called the Golden Jubilee.

Satay Sauce

(naam-jim-satay)

หน้าจิ้มสะเต๊ะ

1 (14-ounce) can coconut milk

2 tablespoons red curry paste

1/2 teaspoon coriander

3/4 teaspoon salt

5 tablespoons sugar or palm sugar

1 tablespoon tamarind juice

1/2 cup ground peanuts

Makes 1 1/2 cups

- Heat the coconut milk in a small saucepan over medium heat until bubbly. Add the curry paste and coriander and whisk until blended. Add the salt, sugar and tamarind juice and stir to combine.
- Add the peanuts and cook for 5 minutes longer. Taste and adjust the seasonings as desired. Satay sauce may be stored in the refrigerator for up to 2 weeks.

Note: To make tamarind juice, mix 1 portion of tamarind pulp to 2 portions of water. Mix well and strain the pulp.

Cucumber Relish

(ah-jahd)

อาจาด

1/4 cup white vinegar

1/4 cup sugar

1/2 teaspoon salt

1 cucumber

1 large shallot, thinly sliced

1 or 2 jalapeño peppers (red and green), thinly sliced

Makes 2 1/2 to 3 cups

- Combine the vinegar, sugar and salt in a bowl and whisk until the sugar is dissolved.
- Peel the cucumber, cut lengthwise into quarters and thinly slice vertically.
- Combine the cucumbers, shallot and jalapeño peppers in a serving bowl and toss with the vinegar mixture.

Note: The vegetables may be cut in advance but wait until serving to add the vinegar mixture.

I have not yet met a person who does not like Pad Thai. This noodle dish has multiple versions. There is the pink version from the street vendor in the market, the brown version that my mom makes seasoned with black soy sauce, and this restaurant version which seems to please all. Buy the skinniest rice noodles you can find; they will double in size once cooked. If served alone, this dish will feed only two hungry adults.

Pad Thai

(pad-thai) ผัดไทย

1 cup thinly sliced pork

1 teaspoon light soy sauce

1/2 (14-ounce) package rice noodles

1/4 cup canola oil

2 large shallots, chopped

1/4 cup sweetened dried radish, chopped

1/4 cup cubed extra-firm tofu (optional)

1/4 cup palm sugar or granulated sugar

1/4 cup fish sauce

1 cup shrimp, shelled and deveined

3 eggs

3 cups bean sprouts

1/2 cup garlic chives

1/4 cup dried shrimp

Lime slices

Dried chili flakes

Fish sauce

Sugar

Roasted peanuts

Serves 2 to 4

- Marinate the pork in the light soy sauce in a bowl for 30 minutes to 1 hour. Soak the rice noodles in warm water in a bowl for 20 minutes; drain.
- Heat the wok over medium-high heat and add the oil. Add the shallots and fry until golden. Add the dried radish, pork and tofu and cook until the pork is crumbly and opaque, stirring constantly.
- Add the noodles, sugar and fish sauce and cook until the noodles are soft. Push the noodles to the side of the wok and add the shrimp. Cook until the shrimp are light pink.
- Push the shrimp to the side with the noodles and add the eggs. Cook until the eggs are scrambled, stirring constantly.
- Stir in the bean sprouts, garlic chives and dried shrimp. Remove from the heat.
- Serve with separate bowls of lime slices, dried chili flakes, fish sauce, sugar and roasted peanuts. Top each serving of noodles with equal amounts of each condiment. For example, add one teaspoon of fish sauce for each teaspoon of sugar. The chili flakes are optional but add great spiciness to the dish. Squeeze the lime over the noodles and discard the rind. Once you have added all the desired condiments, mix well and enjoy! Thai noodles dishes are normally eaten with chopsticks.

- Green onion or regular chives may be substituted for garlic chives.
- The best way to cut the lime is to make three diagonal cuts around the lime. Discard the core.
- When buying fresh bean sprouts, buy only those that are white and clean; avoid the brown discolored sprouts. Bean sprouts need to be aired out so leave the bag open in the refrigerator. The day you plan to use the sprouts, soak the sprouts in cold water and drain just before use.
- Roasting your own peanuts gives a much better aroma and flavor than pre-roasted store-bought brands. Spread the peanuts in a single layer on a baking sheet. Bake at 375 degrees for 8 to 10 minutes or until light brown. Cool completely. Remove the skins of the peanuts by rubbing between your palms. Peanuts may be stored indefinitely in the freezer.

new converts

thai tidbit

Thailand is the only country in Southeast Asia not to be colonized by Western countries. The name "Thailand" means "Land of the Free."

This rich and creamy dessert used to be sold everywhere in Thailand, but it is becoming rarer as Western ice cream becomes popular and more readily available. We eat coconut ice cream with all sorts of toppings, including corn, sticky rice, peanuts, and bread cubes. Actually, the "topping" is served under the ice cream.

Coconut Ice Cream

(ice-a-cream-ga-ti)

ไอศครีมกะทิ

6 cups fresh coconut milk (canned can be substituted)

1½ cups sugar

1 tablespoon vanilla extract

Pinch of salt

Makes 2 quarts

- Heat the coconut milk, sugar, vanilla and salt together in a saucepan over medium-low heat just until bubbles appear along the edge of the pan, stirring constantly to prevent curdling. Remove from the heat immediately and let cool completely. Pour the mixture into in an ice cream freezer and freeze using the manufacturer's directions.
- Spoon into bowls and sprinkle with toasted grated coconut and toasted peanuts. Garnish with a sprig of mint, if desired.

Note: To toast coconut, spread grated coconut on a baking sheet. Bake at 350 degrees for 5 to 8 minutes or until light brown. Traditionally, the Thais cook the coconut milk with bai-tuey (pandanus), a long aromatic leaf used in Thai desserts. This gives fragrance to the ice cream, but it is hard to find. Occasionally, it can be found in the frozen food section of an Oriental market. When thawed it loses some of its fragrance so I substitute vanilla. See the Glossary (page 115) to learn how to make fresh coconut milk.

THAILAND *a view from above*

THAI STYLE

A refreshing drink you can find on almost every street corner: if you buy it in Thailand, make sure to tell them not to add salt. This drink is a summer staple for us in America.

Watermelon Smoothie

(naam-dtaeng-mo-bahn)   หวาแตงโมปั่น

4 cups watermelon chunks, seeded

2 cups ice cubes

4 to 6 tablespoons Simple Syrup (below)

Serves 2

- Combine the watermelon, ice and Simple Syrup in a blender and process until smooth.
- Serve in glasses garnished with mint leaves.

Note: This smoothie is delicious with strawberry, banana or pineapple used separately or combined together.

Simple Syrup

(naam-chuam)   หวาเชื่อม

1 cup sugar

1 cup water

Makes 1¹/4 cups

- Bring the sugar and water to a boil in a sauce pan. Reduce the heat and simmer for 20 minutes, stirring occasionally.
- Cool completely and store in the refrigerator.

thai tidbit

The Thai language is unique. It is comprised of forty-four consonants, five tones, and thirty-two long or short vowels.

traditional dinner

Menu for 6 to 8 people

Fish Cakes with Tangy Cucumber Sauce
Coconut Chicken Soup with Galangal
Beef Panang Curry
Chicken and Cashews
Glass Noodle Salad
Limeade
Sticky Rice and Mangoes

In a Thai kitchen, meals are prepared with these flavors in mind: mild, spicy, sour, salty, and sweet. Along the way, we like to include a vegetable dish and a soup. In this menu, there is more than one spicy dish. You can reduce or augment the amount of chili peppers to your taste. These dishes are served with jasmine rice (see page 51 for Tips on Cooking Rice).

Time-saving tips

One month before
Prepare and shape the fish cakes. You may freeze them before the frying stage and thaw overnight before serving.

One day before
Marinate the meats for all the recipes.

Morning of the dinner
Chop all the vegetables. Make the Beef Panang Curry. Refrigerate and reheat before serving. Prepare the Sticky Rice.

This deep-fried treat has just a touch of spice. It's one of my personal favorites, as an appetizer, a snack, or part of a main dish. I eat it every time I go home to visit my parents. However, don't buy this off the street as it is usually full of red food coloring. If you are lucky enough to find asparagus beans (a.k.a. snake beans or yard-long beans), by all means use them in place of the string beans.

Fish Cakes

(todd-mun-pla)   ทอดมันปลา

2 cups ground fresh catfish fillet

3/4 cup fresh string beans, thinly sliced

6 Kaffir lime leaves, thinly sliced

1 teaspoon white pepper

1/2 teaspoon coriander powder, or
1 tablespoon ground cilantro root

2 tablespoons red curry paste

1 tablespoon fish sauce

Canola oil for deep frying

Makes 20 to 30 two-inch patties

- Combine the catfish, beans, lime leaves, white pepper, coriander powder, red curry paste and fish sauce in a bowl and mix well. Shape the mixture into 2-inch patties.
- Deep fry the patties in 375-degree oil for 1 to 2 minutes or until they rise to the surface of the oil. Turn the patties and fry for 1 to 2 minutes longer or until golden brown.
- Remove the patties with a slotted spoon and drain on paper towels. Serve with Tangy Cucumber Sauce (below).

Note: Most grocery stores remove the cilantro root, so unless you grow your own cilantro, just stick with the coriander powder.

Tangy Cucumber Sauce

(naam-jim)   น้ำจิ้ม

1 garlic clove, chopped

3 to 5 red chili peppers, finely chopped

3 1/2 tablespoons white vinegar

1/4 cup palm sugar or brown sugar

3/4 teaspoon salt

1 cucumber, quartered and thinly sliced

Makes 1 1/4 cups

- Combine the garlic, chili peppers, vinegar, sugar and salt in a small bowl and mix well. Add the cucumber just before serving.

With a mixture of aromatic Thai herbs, this soup is flavorful and zesty without being overpowering—not your usual chicken soup. If you like dry roots, add the galangal powder for optimal flavor; it will make your soup slightly darker in color. Though not found in the traditional recipe, I like the extra flavor from the roasted chili paste and the texture from the mushrooms. This is my husband's favorite soup and my son's preference when he has a cold.

Coconut Chicken Soup with Galangal

(dtom-kah-gai)

3 cups water

2 stalks lemongrass, sliced into 2-inch pieces

6 Kaffir lime leaves

10 slices fresh galangal root, cut into 1/4-inch rounds

2 boneless skinless chicken breasts, thinly sliced

2 (14-ounce) cans coconut milk

1 (15-ounce) can whole straw mushrooms

1/3 cup fish sauce

2 tablespoons roasted chili paste

3 tablespoons lime juice

2 tablespoons chopped Thai chili peppers (optional)

1/4 cup chopped cilantro

Serves 2 to 4

- Combine the water, lemongrass, lime leaves and galangal root in a large saucepan and bring to a boil. Add the chicken and simmer until cooked through.
- Stir in the coconut milk and mushrooms and cook for 5 minutes or until boiling, stirring constantly to prevent curdling. Reduce the heat to medium-low. Add the fish sauce, chili paste and lime juice and mix well. You may add the chili peppers for extra flavor.
- Remove from the heat and sprinkle with the cilantro. Ladle into bowls and serve immediately.

Note: You may substitute dried galangal root. If using the dried root, add 2 teaspoons galangal powder.

thai tidbit

A special vocabulary is reserved for when speaking with royalty.

Most people believe that curry is difficult to make. Actually, it's not! This is a good example of a simple curry. And the flavor improves with time, making it an excellent candidate for leftovers—stunning flavor in under thirty minutes.

Beef Panang Curry

(panang-nua)

พะแนงเนื้อ

1 (14-ounce) can coconut milk

¼ cup panang curry paste

1 pound tender beef, sliced

2 tablespoons sugar

3 tablespoons fish sauce

4 fresh jalapeño peppers, sliced lengthwise

10 fresh Kaffir lime leaves, thinly sliced

1 sprig basil

Serves 2 to 4

- Bring the coconut milk to a boil in a saucepan over medium-high heat. Add the curry paste and stir until blended. Stir in the beef and simmer until the beef is cooked through.
- Add the sugar, fish sauce, and jalapeños and mix well. Cook until the jalapeños are tender-crisp. Stir in the lime leaves and remove from the heat. Garnish with the basil.

Note: Chicken may be substituted for beef in this recipe.

Kaffir lime leaves are a crucial ingredient. Buy as much as you like, as it freezes wonderfully. To thaw the leaves, just rinse with hot water. This dish is still wonderful without the Kaffir lime leaves, but it won't have the authentic panang flavor.

thai tidbit

The traditional Thai New Year is called "Wan-song-kran" day. Thais celebrate by having a huge water fight. Appropriately, the celebration is held in April, the hottest month.

Like most Thai stir-fry dishes, this recipe has Chinese influence with lots of zing from the roasted chili paste and a crunch from water chestnuts. Did you know that cashew nuts do not grow in a shell? They grow in a tree and are attached to a fruit that is shaped like an apple.

Chicken and Cashews

(gai-pad-med-ma-muang)

ไก่ผัดเม็ดมะม่วง

2 boneless skinless chicken breasts, cut into 1/2-inch cubes

1 tablespoon soy sauce

Pinch of white pepper

1/4 cup canola oil

4 garlic cloves, minced

2 tablespoons soy sauce

1 small onion, sliced lengthwise

2 tablespoons oyster sauce

2 tablespoons roasted chili paste

2 tablespoons sugar

3 tablespoons water

1 (4-ounce) can water chestnuts, drained

2 large dried poblano peppers, cut into chunks

1/2 bunch green onion, sliced into 2-inch pieces

1 cup roasted unsalted cashews

Serves 2 to 4

- Combine the chicken, 1 tablespoon of the soy sauce and the white pepper in a shallow dish; set aside.
- Heat the canola oil in a wok over medium-high heat. Add the garlic and cook until golden. Add the chicken and stir-fry until cooked through.
- Add 2 tablespoons soy sauce, the onion, oyster sauce, chili paste and sugar, and stir until combined. Stir in the water and water chestnuts and cook for 2 minutes. Add the dried peppers, green onion and cashews.

When I was growing up, each time my parents hosted a get-together my mother would serve this dish. You will soon find out that Thai salads are quick and easy to make, low in fat, but high in flavor. I call it "guilt-free eating." A great summer side dish, though for me it would make a good lunch, think of it as a Thai pasta salad. Serve it warm or at room temperature.

Glass Noodle Salad

(yum-woon-sen)   ยำวุ้นเส้น

1 (4-ounce) package glass noodles

6 cups boiling water

1/2 cup ground pork

1/2 cup cooked shrimp, peeled and deveined (thaw if frozen)

2 tablespoons lime juice

3 tablespoons fish sauce

Pinch of sugar

1 to 2 teaspoons chili flakes

3 tablespoons chopped green onion

3 tablespoons chopped cilantro

2 shallots, sliced

Thinly sliced cucumbers (optional)

Serves 2

- Cook the glass noodles in boiling water in a saucepan until translucent and soft. Drain the noodles, reserving the water. Rinse in cold water, drain and set aside.
- Cook the pork in the reserved boiling water until opaque and cooked through; drain.
- Combine the noodles, pork, shrimp, lime juice, fish sauce and sugar in a large bowl and mix well. Add the chili flakes, green onion, cilantro and shallots and toss to combine. Serve with cucumber slices, if desired.

Note: If you want to make the dish spicier by adding more chili flakes, remember also to add more fish sauce and lime juice.

Limeade

(naam-ma-nao)   น้ำมะนาว

1/4 cup lime juice

1/2 cup water

6 tablespoons Simple Syrup (page 19)

Serves 1

- Combine the lime juice, water and Simple Syrup in a small bowl and mix well. Serve over crushed ice.

This is everyone's favorite Thai dessert. It's sold primarily during the months of March through May. My husband almost got arrested in Sri Racha trying to buy this dish one night . . . it's too long a story to tell! Search for a flat, yellow-skinned mango. The large round mango doesn't provide the best flavor. A good mango is similar in texture to a ripe peach.

Sticky Rice and Mangoes

(kao-neow-mah-muang)

ข้าวเหนียวมะม่วง

1 (14-ounce) can coconut milk

1/2 cup sugar

3/4 teaspoon salt

4 cups cooked Sticky Rice (page 30)

2 ripe mangoes, thinly sliced

Sesame seeds

Serves 4 to 6

Note: To slice a mango, hold the mango horizontally and peel off the skin with a sharp knife. Starting at one end, cut the mango just above the pit and slice off the flesh in one piece. Flip the mango and repeat the process on the other side. Place the mango halves on a cutting board and cut lengthwise into slices.

- Combine the coconut milk, sugar and salt in a saucepan and bring to a boil over medium heat, stirring constantly. Remove 1/4 cup to a small bowl and set aside for the topping.
- Reduce the heat to low and add the Sticky Rice.
- Cook for 5 to 10 minutes or until all the milk has been absorbed, stirring occasionally. Remove from the heat; the mixture will be very thick.
- Place a mound of sticky rice on each dessert plate and top with mango slices. Drizzle with the reserved coconut milk mixture and sprinkle with sesame seeds.

esaan style for everyone

Sticky Rice
Papaya Salad
Grilled Pork or Beef
Northeastern (Esaan) Beef Salad
Grilled Chicken
Northeastern Chicken Salad
Coconut Flan

Esaan food, from the northeast region of Thailand, is a rising star among both Thais and foreigners. Sticky Rice, the crowning glory of the menu, is beloved by kids and adults alike. Everyone has fun rolling the rice into little balls. Keep a small bowl of water at each place setting to rinse your hands. The children can just eat the grilled chicken or pork if they find the other dishes to be too spicy. Don't let all these spicy dishes scare you away. You can reduce the spice to suit your palate. A rich, creamy, cool dessert, such as Coconut Flan, is the perfect finale to this spicy feast. Try this at your next barbecue.

Time-saving tips

One day before
Marinate the meats for all the recipes. Soak the sticky rice. Mince the chicken for the Northeastern Chicken Salad. Prepare the Coconut Flan and chill.

Morning of the dinner
Make the rice powder by toasting and grinding the uncooked sticky rice. Chop the vegetables. Cook the Sticky Rice for the meal. Complete all preparations.

Thai food uses sticky rice in addition to the typical jasmine rice. This is not just steamed rice that was cooked improperly—it is glutinous rice. Preparing sticky rice takes planning, as it needs to be soaked in water for several hours before cooking.

Sticky Rice

(kao-nee-o)   ข้าวเหนียว

2 cups uncooked sticky rice

Water to cover

Serves 4

- Place the rice in a medium bowl and add enough water to cover. Soak the rice for 2 hours or overnight. Pour the rice into a fine-mesh strainer and rinse until the water runs clear.
- Place the rice in a bamboo steamer and steam over medium-high heat for 20 minutes, or until the rice is translucent. The longer you soak the rice, the less time it will take to cook.
- You may use a rice cooker if you prefer. Place the uncooked rice in the cooker and add enough water to barely cover the rice. Close the lid and cook the rice until the automatic button indicates that it is done. This method of cooking will make softer, messier rice than the steam method.
- To eat sticky rice, roll a small amount in your palm to form a ball. You may use a fork if you wish.

Some of the recipes in this chapter call for rice powder. You may purchase ready-made rice powder in a jar, but you will sacrifice the aroma for convenience. Making your own powder is easier than you may think.

Rice Powder

(kao-kua-pbon)   ข้าวคั่วป่น

1/4 cup uncooked sticky rice or jasmine rice

Makes 2 tablespoons

- Place the rice in a small, dry skillet over medium-high heat. Cook the rice until golden brown, rotating the pan continuously to ensure even browning. A crackling sound indicates that the rice is done. Remove from the heat and cool completely.
- Grind the rice in a blender or coffee grinder until it forms a fine powder. Place in a small jar with a tight-fitting lid and store at room temperature for up to 2 weeks.

This tongue-tingling salad will take your taste buds through the roof, leaving you asking for more. The flavors of garlic and chili peppers cascade through each bite. You can make it as mild as you like, but I prefer it extra spicy. This is by far my favorite salad. I try to eat it every day while I'm in Thailand.

Papaya Salad

(som-tum)

4 to 10 chili peppers (or as many as you like)

2 large garlic cloves, peeled

1/2 cup dried shrimp, rinsed clean

1/2 cup long green beans, cut into 2-inch pieces (optional)

1/2 cup palm sugar

6 tablespoons fish sauce

6 tablespoons lime juice

1 cup cherry tomatoes, halved

1 small green papaya, grated into long strips (makes approximately 4 cups)

1/2 cup unsalted roasted peanuts

Serves 2 to 4

- Place the chili peppers and garlic in a mortar and pound with a pestle until coarsely crushed. Add the dried shrimp and beans and pound lightly.
- Scoop the mixture into a bowl and stir in the palm sugar, fish sauce and lime juice. Taste the mixture to see if the flavors are balanced. Add the tomatoes and papaya and toss until well combined. Sprinkle with the roasted peanuts and serve.

Note: Traditionally, this dish is made with a mortar and pestle. Depending on the size of your mortar, you may have to prepare this dish in two batches. If you don't have a mortar and pestle, just mince the garlic and peppers and mix the ingredients in a bowl.

The palm sugar is crucial to the integrity of the recipe—do not substitute brown sugar.

Pick a firm green papaya with no blemishes and keep it refrigerated until ready to use. If it is soft to the touch, it is too ripe. Grate the papaya with a handheld cheese grater. Wait until close to mealtime to grate the papaya because grated papaya becomes chewy and bitter when stored in the refrigerator.

thai tidbit

A dowry is still required prior to an engagement.

At every school in Thailand, we have all types of snack vendors that congregate just outside the school gate. I remember waiting in line after school for this tasty appetizer. The vendor would place the pork in a cellophane bag and pour sauce over it. Yum, yum! This recipe works well with any cut of meat appropriate for grilling.

Grilled Pork or Beef

(moo-yang, nua-yang)

หมูย่าง – เนื้อย่าง

2 garlic cloves, minced

1 teaspoon white pepper

4 teaspoons soy sauce

2 teaspoons fish sauce

1 tablespoon sugar

1 pound pork tenderloin or beef sirloin

Serves 2 to 4

- Combine the garlic, white pepper, soy sauce, fish sauce and sugar in a large bowl and mix well. Add the pork and marinate for 1 to 8 hours.
- Drain the pork, discarding the marinade.
- Grill over high heat initially to char the outside of the meat. Lower the heat and cook to the desired degree of doneness. Let the meat rest for 10 minutes before slicing.
- Slice and serve with Sticky Rice (page 30) and Spicy Dipping Sauce (below).

Spicy Dipping Sauce

1 teaspoon dried chili flakes

2 tablespoons fish sauce

1 1/2 tablespoons lime juice

Pinch of sugar

1 shallot, thinly sliced

1 tablespoon chopped cilantro

Makes 1/4 cup

- Combine the dried chili flakes, fish sauce, lime juice, sugar, shallot and cilantro in a bowl and mix well. This sauce can be made a couple of hours in advance and kept in the refrigerator. Let stand at room temperature for 15 minutes before serving.

This is a standard dish in the northeastern part of Thailand. It is always eaten with your fingers. The name of the dish translated literally means "beef waterfall." I have often been asked what this means. My guess is that because it is traditionally so fiery hot, it makes you sweat like a waterfall. Don't sweat it—this recipe is not *that* hot.

Northeastern (Esaan) Beef Salad

(nua-naam-tok)

1/2 tablespoon fish sauce

1 pound beef sirloin

2 shallots, thinly sliced

1/4 cup chopped green onions

1/4 cup chopped cilantro

1/2 cup mint leaves

2 tablespoons Rice Powder (page 30)

2 tablespoons fish sauce

2 tablespoons lime juice

Pinch of sugar

1 1/2 teaspoons ground dried chili peppers

Serves 2 to 4

- Rub 1/2 tablespoon fish sauce onto the beef and set aside for 15 minutes.
- Grill the beef over hot coals for 5 to 7 minutes per side for rare, or 7 to 9 minutes for medium rare. Remove from the grill and let rest for 5 minutes; slice thinly. Toss the beef with the green onions, cilantro and mint leaves in a large bowl.
- Combine the Rice Powder, 2 tablespoons fish sauce, the lime juice, sugar and chili peppers in a small bowl and mix well. Pour the Rice Powder mixture over the beef mixture and stir gently to combine.
- Serve with Sticky Rice (page 30) and vegetables such as cucumbers or cabbage.

thai tidbit

Many homes have a "spirit house" in the yard to provide shelter for good spirits inconvenienced by the construction of the home. It is also common to see spirit houses on large construction sites.

This charred but succulent bird gets its flavor from just a few ingredients. Even though it originated in northeastern Thailand, it is enjoyed throughout the country. You can use the chicken breast only, the thighs, the drumsticks, or the whole bird. If you leave the skin on, you'll have moister meat. Without the skin, the meat dries out quickly, so stay near the grill. In the winter, I roast the chicken instead of grilling outdoors.

Grilled Chicken

(gai-yang) ไก่ย่าง

1 garlic head, minced

1 teaspoon white pepper

1/3 cup light soy sauce

3 tablespoons sugar

1 whole chicken, cut into pieces

Serves 4

- Combine the garlic, white pepper, soy sauce and sugar in a bowl and mix well. Add the chicken and marinate for 1 to 8 hours. Drain the chicken, discarding the marinade.
- Grill the chicken over medium-low coals for 8 to 12 minutes per side or until opaque with no trace of pink near the bone.
- Serve with sweet chili dipping sauce and Sticky Rice (page 30). Thai Kitchen's Red Chili Dipping Sauce is very good.

Northeastern Chicken Salad

(laab-gai) ลาบไก่

1 pound ground chicken

1/2 cup water

2 large shallots, thinly sliced

1/4 cup chopped green onions

1/4 cup chopped cilantro

1/2 cup mint leaves

2 tablespoons Rice Powder (page 30)

3 tablespoons fish sauce

2 tablespoons lime juice

11/2 teaspoons dried chili flakes

Serves 2 to 4

- Combine the chicken and water in a skillet over medium-high heat and cook for 8 to 9 minutes or until white; drain.
- Stir in the shallots, green onions, cilantro, mint leaves, Rice Powder, fish sauce, lime juice and dried chili flakes and mix well.
- Serve with Sticky Rice (page 30) and sliced cucumbers.

Note: Turn this salad into a wrap by placing it on napa cabbage leaves. It is equally flavorful with the substitution of other meats such as ground pork, ground beef, or even ground turkey.

This heavenly custard has a subtle touch of coconut and a deep caramel flavor that will caress your palate. Normally I don't have a sweet tooth, but this is my weakness. I like sending the extra custards home with friends; otherwise, I would eat it for breakfast, lunch, and supper. Make this dish two days in advance so it will be thoroughly chilled.

Coconut Flan

CARAMEL

3/4 cup sugar

1/4 cup water

FLAN

1 (14-ounce) can coconut milk

1 1/4 cups milk

5 eggs

3/4 cup sugar

1/8 teaspoon salt

3/4 teaspoon vanilla extract

Makes 8 custards

- *For the caramel,* combine the sugar and water in a saucepan over medium heat. Gently swirl the pan by the handle over the heat. Cook until a clear syrup forms; do not stir. Increase the heat to high and bring the syrup to a boil. Cover the pan tightly and boil for 2 minutes. Uncover the pan and remove from the heat. Let the syrup cool until it begins to darken. Return the pan to the heat and gently swirl the syrup; cook until the syrup turns amber. Pour the syrup immediately into eight 6-ounce custard cups. Tilt the cups to spread the caramel evenly over the bottom.
- *For the flan,* heat the coconut milk and milk in a saucepan over medium heat until steaming. Remove from the heat and let cool slightly. Whisk the eggs, sugar and salt in a bowl until smooth. Add the milk mixture gradually, whisking constantly until the sugar is dissolved. Strain the mixture through a sieve into a clean bowl. Stir in the vanilla.
- Pour the mixture into the caramel-lined cups and place in a 9×13-inch glass baking dish. Fill the dish with boiling water halfway up the sides of the custard cups. Bake at 325 degrees for 45 to 55 minutes, or until the centers are set. Let cool completely. Chill, covered, for 2 days before serving.
- *To serve,* unmold by dipping the cups into hot water for 1 minute. Loosen the edges with a knife and invert onto dessert plates.

satisfying seafood

Spicy Shrimp Soup
Red Snapper with Spicy Red Sauce
Puffed-Crispy Fried Catfish Salad
Crab Fried Rice
Grilled Mixed Seafood
Blueberry Ice Cream Pie

Time-saving tips

One week before
Prepare the ice cream pie and freeze.
Make the blueberry sauce and freeze.

One day before
Cook the rice for the Crab Fried Rice
and chill.

Morning of the dinner
Chop all the vegetables.

I grew up five minutes from the Gulf of Thailand. My elementary school was right next to the beach, and my high school was one block from it. The town's market also has a great view of the beach, so naturally I love seafood. My dad was an avid fisherman. When my sister was young, my brother and I used to go fishing in the sea with him. Mom would bring the portable charcoal grill to the beach, and we would eat whatever Dad caught. Instant seafood barbecues—those are my fondest family memories. Still today, eating seafood brings back special memories of childhood.

This menu combination is truly my favorite. When it comes to grilled seafood, clams, mussels, crabs, and shrimp make a great combination. By now you have discovered that we, the Thais, love spicy things. Don't let that intimidate you. Feel free to reduce the amount of chili peppers or eliminate them altogether. The menu will still hold its tastiness without the heat.

This soup is not for the faint-hearted. The Thai people love this soup—the hotter, the better. It's not a soothing, comforting kind of soup, but it is addictive. The more you eat, the more you want! The sourness combined with the spiciness can really clear up any sinus problems. You may add additional chili peppers if you want to increase the heat. Just be sure to keep a box of tissues around!

Spicy Shrimp Soup

satisfying seafood

(dtom-yum-gung)

ต้มยำกุ้ง

6 cups shrimp stock (see Note below)

8 Kaffir lime leaves

2 stalks lemongrass, sliced into 2-inch pieces

1 pound shrimp with tails on, peeled and deveined (reserve the shells for stock)

1 (15-ounce) can whole straw mushrooms

3 tablespoons roasted chili paste

1/4 cup fish sauce

1 tablespoon (or more) chopped chili peppers

3 tablespoons lime juice

1/4 cup chopped cilantro

Serves 2 to 4

- Bring the stock, lime leaves and lemongrass to a boil in a stockpot over high heat.
- Add the shrimp, mushrooms, chili paste and fish sauce and stir to combine. Cook for 5 minutes or until the shrimp are pink. Remove from the heat. Stir in the chili peppers, lime juice and cilantro.
- Ladle into bowls and garnish with additional cilantro, if desired.

Note: To make the shrimp stock, combine 7 cups of water and the reserved shrimp shells in a stockpot. Bring to a boil over medium heat. Reduce the heat and simmer for 10 minutes. Drain and discard the shells. You may keep the stock, covered, in the refrigerator for 2 to 3 days.

thai tidbit

In Thailand, it's impolite to point your foot at anyone or anything.

Another quick and easy dish to prepare, this is a great example of multiple tastes in one bite: sweet, salty, sour, and spicy. You must try this recipe if you are looking for new energy in a fish dish.

Red Snapper with Spicy Red Sauce

(pla-raad-prik)

ปลาราดพริก

RED SNAPPER

2 cups canola oil

1 whole red snapper, scales removed and fish cleaned, or 2 red snapper fillets

SPICY RED SAUCE

2 tablespoons canola oil

4 shallots, finely minced

6 garlic cloves, finely minced

6 fresh Thai chili peppers

1½ tablespoons fish sauce

3 tablespoons palm sugar

1½ tablespoons tamarind juice

2 tablespoons water

Serves 2

- *For the snapper,* heat the oil to 375 degrees in a large heavy-bottomed saucepan or deep fryer. Lower the snapper gently into the hot oil and deep-fry for 5 minutes per side or until golden brown. Remove from the oil and drain on a paper towel-lined plate. Place on a platter and keep warm.
- *For the sauce,* heat the oil in a saucepan over medium heat. Add the shallots, garlic and chili peppers and stir-fry for 2 minutes. Add the fish sauce, palm sugar, tamarind juice and water and mix well. Bring the mixture to a boil and cook for 2 minutes. Remove from the heat. Pour the sauce over the snapper and serve.

thai tidbit

All Westerners are called "farangs" by the Thai people.

A well-loved salad among seafood eaters, this is another sour-spicy refreshing salad with an extra crunch from frying the grilled catfish. For a lighter version of this dish, you may simply grill the fish and skip the frying: you'll lose the crunch but not the flavor. While the catfish is grilling, you can prepare the mango salad.

Puffed-Crispy Fried Catfish Salad

(yum-pla-dook-fu)

ย่ำปลาดุกฟู

1 large catfish, or 2 catfish fillets

4 cups canola oil

1 cup green mango, grated

1 shallot, thinly sliced

2 chili peppers, thinly sliced

3 tablespoons fish sauce

2 tablespoons lime juice

3 tablespoons palm sugar

Serves 2

- Grill the catfish over hot coals for 5 minutes per side or until the flesh turns white. Let cool slightly and shred into small pieces.
- Heat the oil to 375 degrees in a large heavy saucepan or deep fryer. Add the grilled catfish pieces and deep fry until puffed and golden. Remove from the oil and drain on paper towels. Arrange the fried catfish pieces on a platter and set aside.
- Combine the mango, shallot, chili peppers, fish sauce, lime juice and palm sugar in a bowl and mix well. Spoon the mango mixture over the fried catfish and serve immediately.

thai tidbit

In Thailand, you must never walk over anyone who is lying down on the floor.

This is a must at any Thai seafood restaurant. It's usually reserved for special occasions because crab is expensive. However, with the availability of frozen crab meat, you can make this as often as you wish.

Crab Fried Rice

(kao-pahd-bpu) | ข้าวผัดปู

5 tablespoons canola oil

1 small onion, chopped

1 cup cooked crab meat (drain if frozen)

3 eggs, lightly beaten

6 cups cooked rice

1/2 teaspoon white pepper

3 tablespoons fish sauce

1 1/2 tablespoons sugar

2 green onions, chopped

1/4 cup chopped cilantro

Cucumber slices

Serves 2 to 4

- Heat a wok over medium-high heat. Add the oil and heat until shimmering. Add the onion and stir-fry for 2 to 3 minutes or until translucent. Stir in the crab meat and push the mixture to one side of the wok.
- Add the eggs and cook until scrambled, stirring constantly. Add the rice, white pepper, fish sauce and sugar and mix well. Stir in the green onions and remove from the heat.
- Sprinkle the cilantro over the rice and serve immediately with cucumber slices.

Note: Thais love cucumber, as it complements the rice very well. If you like, squeeze some lime juice on your rice before eating. We also like to add peppers.

thai tidbit

Instead of shaking hands, the Thais greet each other with a "wai," a graceful bringing together of the hands in a prayer-like manner.

The secret is not the fish, but the sauce. Transform your typical grilled summer food into an exotic tropical getaway. Your guests will thank you and you will soon have the most popular grill in the neighborhood. Grilling seafood is just like grilling chicken or beef, it just requires less time.

Grilled Mixed Seafood

(ahan-taleh-yang)

อาหารทะเลย่าง

8 pounds assorted seafood of your choice: shrimp, mussels, clams, lobster

Serves 6 to 8

- Lobster will take the most time, about 15 minutes. Grill over hot coals until the lobster meat is opaque.
- Grill the mussels and clams for 10 minutes or until the shells open.
- Grill the shrimp over hot coals for 5 minutes, turning once, or until the flesh turns pink.

Seafood Dipping Sauce

(naam-jim-taleh)

น้ำจิ้มทะเล

5 to 10 fresh Thai chili peppers, finely chopped

5 garlic cloves, minced

3/4 teaspoon salt

1/4 cup lime juice

1/4 cup palm sugar

Makes 1/2 cup

- Combine the chili peppers, garlic, salt, lime juice and palm sugar in a bowl and mix well. Let sit at room temperature until ready to use. This recipe can easily be doubled or tripled, according to the amount of seafood you are grilling.

When Dennis and I were dating and lived in Bangkok, we would often order this dessert at S&P Restaurant. That's what inspired me to create this simple ice cream dessert. You may want to change the topping to strawberry or even chocolate, but we like it just the way it is.

Blueberry Ice Cream Pie

CRUST

¹/₃ cup (²/₃ stick) butter, melted

¹/₄ cup sugar

Pinch of salt

1¹/₂ cups graham cracker crumbs

FILLING

1 quart vanilla ice cream, slightly softened

BLUEBERRY SAUCE

1 (16-ounce) package frozen blueberries

¹/₂ cup sugar

¹/₂ cup water

1¹/₂ tablespoons cornstarch

2 tablespoons orange juice

Serves 8

- *For the crust,* combine the butter, sugar, salt, and graham cracker crumbs in a bowl and mix well. Press the mixture evenly over the bottom and up the side of a 9-inch pie plate. Bake at 375 degrees for 5 minutes or until the edges are light brown. Let cool completely before filling.
- *For the filling,* spread the ice cream into the cooled crust. Freeze until firm. This can be made up to one month in advance and frozen, covered with plastic wrap, until ready to serve.
- *For the sauce,* combine the blueberries, sugar, water, cornstarch and orange juice in a heavy saucepan over medium-high heat. Cook until bubbly, stirring frequently. Reduce the heat and simmer for 15 minutes. Remove from the heat and let cool. Pour into a jar with a tight-fitting lid and refrigerate for up to 1 week.
- Remove the pie from the freezer 30 minutes before serving.
- *To serve,* place a slice of pie on a dessert plate and pour ¹/₄ cup of the blueberry sauce over the top.

thai lunch box

Beef and Mushrooms in Oyster Sauce
Beef with Bell Peppers
Pork with Holy Basil
Chicken Fried Rice
Fried Mussels Pancake with Bean Sprouts

In Thailand, our breakfast, lunch, and supper are really quite the same. We can eat them at any time. Though the following dishes are some I would normally order along with additional dishes, you may use any of these recipes by themselves for dinner. Most of these dishes, with the exceptions of Fried Mussels Pancake and Beef with Bell Peppers, can be interchanged with pork, chicken, or beef. That's what makes stir-frying so versatile. In school, Thai children bring their lunches in a three-tier stackable stainless steel container. Rice is in one tier and two main dishes in the others. This is how I took my lunch to school while in junior high.

Time-saving tips

One day before
Cook the rice for the fried rice and refrigerate. Clean the mussels and remove them from their shells; refrigerate. Slice the beef for the two beef dishes. Slice the chicken for the fried rice.

Morning of the dinner
Chop the vegetables for all the dishes. Prepare the Chicken Fried Rice; you may warm it up just before serving.

Thirty minutes before
Stir-fry all the dishes.

This is one of the mildest dishes that you will find in this book. The tender beef and chewy mushrooms mingle perfectly in the velvety smooth sauce. It's necessary to use a tender cut of beef like tenderloin or tip sirloin. Any combination of mushrooms will be wonderful. I particularly love oyster mushrooms in this dish.

Beef and Mushrooms in Oyster Sauce

(nua-pad-naam-man-hoy-gup-het)

เนื้อผัดน้ำมันหอยกับเห็ด

1 teaspoon soy sauce

Pinch of sugar

Pinch of pepper

1/2 teaspoon cornstarch

1 cup sliced beef sirloin

3 tablespoons canola oil

2 garlic cloves, minced

2 cups sliced button mushrooms or mixed wild mushrooms, cut into pieces

2 tablespoons oyster sauce

1 tablespoon sugar

1/2 cup Thai Stock (page 85) or water

3 green onions, cut into 2-inch pieces

Serves 2

- Combine the soy sauce, pinch of sugar, pepper and cornstarch in a bowl and mix well. Add the beef and marinate for 1 hour.
- Heat the oil in a wok over medium-high heat until shimmering. Add the garlic and stir-fry until golden. Add the beef and stir-fry for 3 minutes or to the desired degree of doneness. Stir in the mushrooms, oyster sauce, 1 tablespoon sugar, and the stock and cook until bubbly. Stir in the green onions and remove from the heat.

thai tidbit

Thailand was known as Siam until 1939.

A more familiar name might be pepper steak. This dish gets its appealing color from two kinds of bell peppers. My husband frequently ordered this dish in restaurants when we were dating.

Beef with Bell Peppers

(nua-pad-prik-yai)

เนื้อผัดพริกใหญ่

2 teaspoons cornstarch

1 teaspoon light soy sauce

Pinch of white pepper

1 teaspoon sugar

2 cups sliced tender beef

1/4 cup canola oil

2 garlic cloves, minced

2 tablespoons soy sauce

2 tablespoons oyster sauce

2 tablespoons sugar

1 green bell pepper, cut into 1-inch pieces

1 red bell pepper, cut into 1-inch pieces

1 onion, cut into 1-inch pieces

1/4 cup Thai Stock (page 85) or water

Serves 2

- Combine the cornstarch, 1 teaspoon light soy sauce, the white pepper and 1 teaspoon sugar in a bowl and mix well. Add the beef and toss to coat evenly. Marinate for 5 minutes.
- Heat the oil in the wok until shimmering. Add the garlic and stir-fry until golden.
- Add the beef and stir-fry for 3 minutes or to the desired degree of doneness. Stir in 2 tablespoons soy sauce, the oyster sauce, 2 tablespoons sugar, the bell peppers, onion and stock. Stir-fry for 2 to 3 minutes longer, or until the bell peppers are tender-crisp.

thai tidbit

In most cities in Thailand, the national anthem is played over loudspeakers at 8:00 a.m. and 6:00 p.m. All public activity is expected to pause until the song is over.

This is one of Thailand's most popular "made-to-order" dishes. It's not just for lunch, either—my mom would make this for breakfast! The heat of the holy basil and the fire from the peppers would really wake us up.

Pork with Holy Basil

(gra-pao-mu)

กระเพราหมู

3 tablespoons canola oil

4 garlic cloves, minced

6 Thai chili peppers

2 cups thinly sliced pork

1/2 tablespoon light soy sauce

1 tablespoon fish sauce

1/2 tablespoon oyster sauce

1 tablespoon sugar

3 tablespoons water

1/2 cup holy basil leaves

Pinch of white pepper

Serves 2

- Heat the oil in a wok over medium-high heat until shimmering. Add the garlic and chili peppers and stir-fry until the garlic turns golden. Add the pork and stir-fry until opaque and cooked through. Stir in the light soy sauce, fish sauce, oyster sauce, sugar and water.
- Toss in the basil and pepper and remove from the heat.

Note: This dish is equally delicious with shrimp, calamari, chicken or beef.

It's rare to find fresh holy basil at oriental grocery stores; I recommend growing your own. When I lived in Texas it grew so big that it became a bush. Look for it in the freezer section. Sometimes you can find the leaves in a pre-made sauce in a jar. If you use the sauce, adjust the seasonings accordingly. See the Glossary (page 114) for more information on basils.

thai tidbit

It is common in Thailand for the recipient of a wedding invitation to return the card with money enclosed.

I never thought that fried rice was exciting until I moved to the United States. I now have a new sense of appreciation of this standby dish. Mix some meat and vegetables into leftover rice, and you have an easy main dish for the whole family. I prefer to use leftover jasmine rice as it produces a softer, fluffier rice. This attractive dish gets its color from tomatoes and green onions.

Chicken Fried Rice

(khao-pahd-gai) ข้าวผัดไก่

1 cup sliced boneless skinless chicken breast

1 teaspoon light soy sauce

3 tablespoons canola oil

4 garlic cloves, chopped

1 onion, sliced lengthwise

3 eggs, lightly beaten

6 cups cooked rice

3 tablespoons soy sauce

2 tablespoons sugar

1/2 teaspoon white pepper

1 Roma tomato, sliced lengthwise

2 green onions, chopped

1/2 cucumber, sliced

Serves 2

- Combine the chicken and light soy sauce in a bowl and set aside.
- Heat a wok over medium heat. Add the oil and heat until shimmering. Add the garlic and stir-fry until golden brown. Add the chicken and onion and stir-fry until the chicken is cooked through.
- Add the eggs and cook until scrambled. Stir in the rice, soy sauce, sugar and pepper and mix well. Add the tomato and green onion and stir to combine. Remove from the heat.
- Serve with cucumber slices on the side.

Note: Pork, beef, or shrimp may be substituted for chicken in this dish.

thai tidbit

Texas is slightly larger than Thailand, which is located halfway across the world from the United States.

Whether at a food court or a night bazaar, where there is Pad Thai, there is hoi-todd. It's like an oversized savory crunchy fritter. If you cannot find fresh mussels, you may substitute oysters. The hardest part of this dish is getting the mussel meat out of the shell. It takes some patience, but with practice you'll be able to shuck the mussels like a Thai. To be on the safe side, remove the meat from the shell the day before and refrigerate. Once the mussels are ready, this dish will take less than thirty minutes to prepare.

Fried Mussels Pancake with Bean Sprouts

(hoi-todd)

หอยทอด

1/2 cup cornstarch

1/2 cup all-purpose flour

2 1/4 cups water

1/4 to 1/3 cup canola oil

1 cup fresh mussels, shelled and bearded

4 eggs

4 garlic cloves, minced

4 cups bean sprouts

1/2 cup Chinese chives or green onions, cut into 2-inch pieces

1 teaspoon white pepper

3 tablespoons fish sauce

1 1/2 tablespoons sugar

Serves 2

- Combine the cornstarch, flour and water together in a bowl and mix well.
- Heat the oil in a cast-iron skillet over medium-high heat. Add 1/2 of the cornstarch mixture to the skillet and scatter the mussels on top. Add the remaining cornstarch mixture to the skillet and cook until golden and crispy, turning once.
- Break the pancake into small pieces. Break the eggs over the pancake pieces and scramble together. Add the garlic and cook until golden. Stir in the bean sprouts, Chinese chives, white pepper, fish sauce and sugar and mix well.
- Spoon the mixture onto plates and sprinkle with cilantro and green onions before serving. Serve with Sriracha sauce (see the Glossary, page 119).

thai tidbit

The telegraph is still a common form of communication in Thailand.

Tips on Cooking Rice

- Most Thai homes have an electric rice cooker. It's a convenient and quick way to cook rice. It's so easy that even my husband knows how to make rice. Just add the same ratio of water and rice; for example, 1 cup of water for 1 cup of rice. Inside the rice cooker, there are lines marking the amount of rice and water. One cup in this case refers to the small plastic measuring cup that comes with the rice cooker. If you enjoy eating Asian food, I suggest that you purchase a rice cooker, which can be found at any oriental grocery and at many department stores. I buy Thai jasmine rice in 25-pound bags at an oriental grocery store, though you can also purchase it in 5-pound bags. You can freeze uncooked rice in a freezer bag; there is no need to thaw it before cooking.

- If you don't have a rice cooker, don't despair. Bring 2 cups of water to a boil in a saucepan and add 1 cup of rice. Cover and simmer for 15 minutes or until the water is absorbed. Cooking rice requires a little bit of experimenting, as each brand of rice requires different amounts of water.

thai tidbit

When eating Thai food, we use the spoon and fork simultaneously. Place the spoon in your predominant hand. With your other hand, push the food onto your spoon using the back side of your fork.

vegetarians only

Fried Tofu with Dipping Sauce
Corn Cakes with Spicy Cucumber Sauce
Stir-Fried Mixed Vegetables
Green Curry with Mushrooms
Grilled Eggplant Salad
Pineapple Napoleons

I enjoy meatless dishes at least three to four times a week. In addition to the recipes found in this chapter, feel free to omit the meat from most dishes that contain vegetables. And vice versa, you can add meat to these recipes to obtain some extra protein in your diet. For all the vegetarians out there, I hope you will give this menu two thumbs-up. Each recipe in this chapter (with the exception of Pineapple Napoleons) is quick and easy.

Time-saving tips

Three days before
Make the caramelized pineapple and chill. Make the mixture for the corn cakes.

Morning of the dinner
Chop all the vegetables.
Bake the puff pastry.

Afternoon of the dinner
Make the Dipping Sauce, Spicy Cucumber Sauce, and Pineapple Sauce and chill. Prepare the Green Curry with Mushrooms; reheat before serving. Grill the eggplant.

I know it sounds crazy, but this is a favorite with my nine-year old son. I think it's the dipping sauce that he really enjoys. Because tofu is very bland, it takes a strong-flavored sauce to tickle your palate. Make sure you use extra-firm tofu. It looks like a square disk rather than a square block. Sometimes it's also called dried bean curd.

Fried Tofu

(thao-hoo-tot)

เต้าหู้ทอด

4 pieces extra-firm tofu

Canola oil for deep-frying

Serves 2

- Heat the oil to 375 degrees in a wok or a large, deep skillet. Add the tofu to the hot oil and fry until golden on both sides; drain on paper towels.
- Slice each piece of tofu into 4 or 5 smaller pieces. Serve with Dipping Sauce (below).

Dipping Sauce

(naam-jim-thao-who)

น้ำจิ้มเต้าหู้

3 large garlic cloves, minced

3 red chili peppers, crushed

2¹/2 tablespoons white vinegar

³/4 teaspoon salt

¹/4 cup palm sugar

¹/4 cup chopped cilantro

¹/4 cup chopped peanuts

Makes ²/3 cup

- Combine the garlic, chili peppers, vinegar, salt and palm sugar in a bowl and mix well. Stir in the cilantro and peanuts. Serve with the tofu.

Variation: I also like to eat the tofu plain, without its being fried. You can steam it in a saucepan until warm or heat it in a microwave. Serve with the Dipping Sauce.

Even if you're not a vegetarian you'll enjoy these satisfying, peppery corn cakes. I use whole eggs as a binding agent, but you may use just the egg whites. If you choose not to use any eggs, you will need to brown the corn cakes in a skillet instead of deep-frying. You must use fresh corn kernels; canned corn does not provide enough starch.

Corn Cakes with Spicy Cucumber Sauce

(todd-man-kao-poad) | ทอดมันข้าวโพด

2 cups fresh corn kernels (2 to 3 ears of corn)

1/2 teaspoon coriander

1 teaspoon finely chopped garlic

1 teaspoon white pepper

1/4 cup each cornstarch and all-purpose flour

1/2 teaspoon salt

2 eggs, or 3 egg whites

2 tablespoons red curry paste

Canola oil for deep-frying

Makes 24 (2-inch) corn cakes

- Combine the corn, coriander, garlic, white pepper, cornstarch, flour, salt, eggs and curry paste in a large bowl and mix well. If you are making this in advance, you may refrigerate the mixture at this point.
- Heat the oil in a heavy saucepan or deep fryer to 375 degrees. Gently drop 2 tablespoons of the corn mixture into the hot oil and fry until golden. Turn over and fry for an additional 1 to 2 minutes or until it floats.
- Drain on paper towels and serve with Spicy Cucumber Sauce (below).

Spicy Cucumber Sauce

3 tablespoons white vinegar

1/4 cup sugar

3/4 teaspoon salt

1 cayenne pepper, chopped

1/4 cup peanuts, chopped

1/2 cucumber, sliced and quartered

Makes about 1 1/2 cups

- Combine the vinegar, sugar and salt in a bowl and stir until the sugar and salt have dissolved. Stir in the cayenne pepper, peanuts and cucumber. Pour into a serving bowl.

This is my favorite combination of vegetables. In Thailand, collard greens are picked very young, making the vegetable tender and less bitter. If you go to an oriental grocery store you will find a smaller version called Chinese broccoli. Feel free to experiment and use whatever combination of vegetables suits your palate. Remember to cook the hard vegetables first, as they take longer to cook, and the soft leaves last.

Stir-Fried Mixed Vegetables

(pat-pak-ruam-mit)

ผัดผักรวมมิตร

1/3 cup Thai Stock (page 85) or water

1 tablespoon cornstarch

1/4 cup canola oil

4 garlic cloves, minced

1/2 cup sliced carrots

1 cup baby corn (fresh or frozen)

1 cup snow peas, trimmed

1 red bell pepper, cut into 1-inch pieces

1 small bunch of asparagus, trimmed and cut into 1-inch pieces

2 cups collard greens, cut into bite-size pieces

1 tablespoon light soy sauce

3 tablespoons oyster sauce

2 tablespoons sugar

Pinch of white pepper

2 cups napa cabbage, cut into bite-size pieces

Serves 2 to 4

- Combine the stock and cornstarch in a small bowl and mix well; set aside.
- Heat the wok over medium-high heat. Add the oil and heat until shimmering. Add the garlic and stir-fry until golden. Add the carrots and cook for 2 minutes, stirring constantly. Add the baby corn, snow peas, bell pepper and asparagus and stir-fry for 2 minutes longer.
- Add the collard greens, soy sauce, oyster sauce, sugar, and pepper. Stir in the stock mixture and cook until bubbly. Stir in the napa cabbage and cook until almost wilted, stirring constantly.

thai tidbit

In Thailand, it is impolite to wear black to
weddings or red to funerals.

You won't even miss the presence of meat in this curry. The mushrooms (such as portobello, crimini, and oyster) provide a chewy texture and meaty flavor that will fool your palate. You'll get the same intense spiciness as regular green curry. Mushrooms only take a short amount of time to cook, making this a quick dish to prepare.

Green Curry with Mushrooms

(gaeng-kio-wan-hed)

แกงเขียวหวานเห็ด

2 (14-ounce) cans coconut milk

4 to 6 tablespoons green curry paste

1 cup water

1 cup green cluster eggplant or green peas

1 cup bamboo shoots

4 jalapeño peppers (both red and green), thinly sliced lengthwise

6 Kaffir lime leaves

8 cups assorted wild or purchased mushrooms

1/3 cup fish sauce

1/4 cup sugar

1 cup basil leaves

Serves 2 to 4

- Heat 1 can of the coconut milk in a large sauce pan over medium high heat until boiling.
- Add the curry paste and stir to combine. Add the remaining can of coconut milk, water, eggplant, bamboo shoots, jalapeño peppers and lime leaves and mix well.
- Stir in the mushrooms, fish sauce and sugar and mix well. Cook for 5 minutes, stirring occasionally. Remove from the heat and stir in the basil leaves.

Note: Green cluster eggplant are a small variety of Thai eggplant. They resemble a bunch of grapes, though slighly smaller in size. Remove the eggplant from the cluster before measuring. If you cannot find green cluster eggplant at your local Asian grocery, check online at www.melissas.com. You may substitute green peas.

thai tidbit

The tooth fairy doesn't come to Thailand. If you lose a bottom tooth, you are to throw it to the rooftop, and if you lose a top tooth, you are to throw it to the ground. Otherwise, the new tooth might not grow.

It took me a while to like eggplant. In fact, it was not until I got married and moved far away from home. I used to think they were just mushy and bland, but not anymore. Eggplant preserves the flavor of the dish with its absorbing characteristics. Look for Japanese eggplant, which is long and slender. A good eggplant should be smooth and firm. This dish is an excellent way to eat eggplant.

Grilled Eggplant Salad

(yum-ma-kua-yow)

ยำมะเขือยาว

4 long Japanese eggplant

3 shallots, thinly sliced

3 chili peppers, sliced

3 tablespoons chopped cilantro

3 tablespoons chopped green onions

2 tablespoons lime juice

2 tablespoons fish sauce

1 tablespoon palm sugar

Leaf lettuce

Serves 2

- Grill the eggplant over hot coals or broil 4 inches from the heat source until the flesh is soft and the skin is brown. Let cool. Remove and discard the skin and cut the flesh into chunks.
- Combine the eggplant, shallots, chili peppers, cilantro and green onions in a large bowl and mix well. Add the lime juice, fish sauce and palm sugar and toss to combine. Serve the eggplant salad on a bed of lettuce.

Note: For non-vegetarians, you may add 1/4 cup cooked ground pork, 1/4 cup cooked shrimp and 1/2 tablespoon each of lime juice, fish sauce and palm sugar.

thai tidbit

It is bad luck for a Thai man to walk under a clothesline that has skirts or underwear hanging to dry.

No need to worry about cutting or seeding your fresh pineapple for this recipe because canned pineapple will work just fine. The pineapple is cooked to a sweet and slightly tender texture. When combined with a store-bought puff pastry, this easy recipe becomes even more of a snap to prepare.

Pineapple Napoleons

PINEAPPLE SAUCE

2 (20-ounce) cans pineapple chunks, drained

1 cup sugar

2 tablespoons rum

1/2 teaspoon cinnamon

PASTRY

1 sheet frozen puff pastry

1 egg, beaten

Whipped topping, or freshly whipped cream

Serves 6

- *For the sauce,* combine the pineapple, sugar, rum and cinnamon in a heavy saucepan over medium-high heat. Bring the mixture to a boil. Reduce the heat and simmer for 25 minutes, or until the pineapple is translucent and the sauce is of a thick syrup consistency, stirring occasionally. You may store the sauce in the refrigerator up to one week—just warm it up before use.
- *For the pastry,* thaw the puff pastry using the package directions. Unfold the pastry and cut into thirds vertically. Cut each third into fourths horizontally; you will end up with 12 rectangles. Brush the pastry with the egg and arrange on a baking sheet.
- Bake at 400 degrees for 15 minutes or until golden brown.
- *To serve,* place one piece of pastry on a serving plate and spoon pineapple sauce over it. Place another puff pastry on top and spoon more pineapple sauce over it. Garnish with a dollop of whipped cream.

curry in a hurry

Mussamun Beef Curry
Spicy Ground Beef with Green Beans
Yellow Chicken Curry
Green Chicken Curry
Dad's Burmese Curry
Fried Ice Cream Balls with Caramel Sauce

I'll be honest with you. I don't make my own curry pastes. I find it to be complicated due to hard-to-find ingredients such as fresh Kaffir limes, of which we use just the rind. And fresh galangal, while it is available, is often expensive. Even in Thailand, most women buy ready-made curry paste. I recommend purchasing a good can of curry paste and adding more spices. With the exception of coconut milk in a can, I use the freshest quality ingredients I can find. And the results are more than acceptable!

Not only are these recipes easy, they also make great leftovers. If you decide to have a curry dinner party, you can easily make these dishes in advance and warm them up the day of your dinner. Even the dessert, Fried Ice Cream Balls, can be warmed and served as a refreshing finale.

Time-saving tips

One month before
Prepare the ice cream balls and freeze. Make Dad's Burmese curry paste and freeze; thaw before using.

Two days before
Make the Yellow Chicken Curry and refrigerate. Make the Mussamun Beef Curry and refrigerate; reheat before serving. Make Dad's Burmese Curry and refrigerate; reheat before serving. Slice the chicken for the Green Chicken Curry.

Morning of the dinner
Prepare the Spicy Ground Beef with Green Beans. Prepare the Green Chicken Curry; wait and add the basil just before serving.

One hour before
Cook the rice and keep warm.

This aromatic Muslim curry is made only with chicken or beef, whichever you prefer. The result is a very tender meat. You may also use a more affordable cut of meat, such as stew meat, for this recipe.

Mussamun Beef Curry

(mussamun-nua)

มัสมั่นเนื้อ

1 tablespoon coriander seeds

5 cardamom pods

2 cinnamon sticks

2 (14-ounce) cans coconut milk

1/4 cup mussamun curry paste

1 large potato, cut into quarters

1 pound beef, cut into 2-inch cubes

1 cup water

1 cup fresh pineapple chunks, or
1 (20-ounce) can pineapple chunks

1/3 cup fish sauce

1/4 cup sugar

2 tablespoons tamarind juice

1/4 cup roasted unsalted peanuts

Serves 2 to 4

- Place the coriander seeds, cardamom pods and cinnamon sticks in a small saucepan over medium heat. Toast the spices, tilting the pan occasionally, until the coriander seeds begin to pop. Remove from the heat and set aside to cool. Grind the spices in a coffee grinder until fine.
- Bring the coconut milk to a boil in a saucepan over medium-high heat. Add the curry paste, ground spices, potato, beef, water, pineapple, fish sauce, sugar and tamarind juice and mix well.
- Cover and reduce the heat. Cook for 30 minutes, or until the potato and beef are tender, stirring occasionally. Sprinkle with the peanuts and serve immediately.

Note: If you use canned pineapple, don't drain the juice. Use it in place of the water.

thai tidbit

It is not common for married couples to
wear wedding rings.

One reason I love this dry-spicy curry is because it requires no coconut milk, and it only takes about fifteen minutes to make. This recipe works well with ground pork or even ground fresh white fish.

Spicy Ground Beef with Green Beans

(pad-ped-prik-king-nua) | ผัดเผ็ดพริกขิงเนื้อ

3 tablespoons canola oil

1/4 cup red curry paste

1 pound ground beef

2 cups green beans

1/4 cup each fish sauce and water

3 tablespoons sugar

2 tablespoons finely cut Kaffir lime leaves

Serves 2 to 4

- Heat the oil in a wok over medium-high heat until shimmering. Add the curry paste and mix well. Add the beef and stir to coat with the curry mixture. Cook for 5 minutes or until the meat is brown and crumbly, stirring often.
- Cut the beans diagonally into 2-inch pieces.
- Add the beans, fish sauce, water and sugar to the beef mixture and mix well. Cook, covered, for 7 to 8 minutes or until the beans are tender-crisp. Stir in the lime leaves.

Yellow Chicken Curry

(gaeng-ga-ri-gai) | แกงกะหรี่ไก่

2 (14-ounce) cans coconut milk

4 to 6 tablespoons yellow curry paste

1 tablespoon curry powder

2 boneless skinless chicken breasts

2 potatoes, cut into quarters

1 large onion, cut into quarters

1/3 cup fish sauce

1/4 cup sugar

Serves 2 to 4

- Place the coconut milk in a medium saucepan and bring to a boil over medium-high heat. Add the curry paste and curry powder and mix well.
- Slice the chicken into thin strips. Add the chicken, potatoes and 1 cup water to the curry mixture and cook for 5 minutes.
- Reduce the heat and add the onion, fish sauce and sugar. Simmer, covered, for 30 minutes, or until the potatoes are tender and the chicken is cooked through, stirring occasionally.

When I'm home, this is the first dish I request from my mom when I get off the airplane. We usually serve it with a special freshly made rice noodle (kanome-jine). There are also vegetable condiments that we place on top of the curry, such as sliced cucumbers, pickled cabbage, chopped yard-long beans, or extra basil. I prefer cucumbers and pickled cabbage.

Green Chicken Curry

(gaeng-kiow-wan-gai)

แกงเขียวหวานไก่

2 (14-ounce) cans coconut milk

1/4 cup green curry paste

2 boneless skinless chicken breasts, thinly sliced

5 white Thai eggplant, halved (optional)

1 cup green cluster eggplant or green peas

1 (14-ounce) can sliced bamboo shoots

4 red and green jalapeño peppers, thinly sliced lengthwise

8 Kaffir lime leaves

1 cup water

1/3 cup fish sauce

1/4 cup sugar

1 cup sweet basil or Thai basil

Serves 2 to 4

- Place the coconut milk in a saucepan and bring to a boil over medium-high heat. Add the curry paste and mix well. Add the chicken and boil for 5 minutes or until cooked through.
- Reduce the heat and add the eggplant, bamboo shoots, jalapeño peppers, lime leaves and water. Simmer, covered, for 10 minutes, stirring occasionally.
- Stir in the fish sauce and sugar. Remove from the heat and stir in the basil.

Note: White Thai eggplant are the size of limes; they are white with thin green vertical stripes. Remove the stems and slice in half.

See page 57 for Note on green cluster eggplant.

thai tidbit

On the day of a wedding, people are very careful not to break anything, as that means the wedding will be cursed.

My dad worked as a spy for the Thai government when I was a child. This recipe is some of the best intelligence he gathered from our Burmese neighbors! The Burmese use salt for seasoning instead of fish sauce, but we Thais prefer the flavor from fish sauce. Be sure you have plenty of ventilation in your kitchen, as the initial mix of hot oil and curry paste can be suffocating. Once you add the other ingredients, the smokiness will subside.

Dad's Burmese Curry

(gaeng-gai-pama)

แกงไก่พม่า

CURRY PASTE

3 large shallots

5 garlic cloves

6 to 10 dried chili peppers

2 teaspoons shrimp paste

3 tablespoons curry powder

CHICKEN

¼ cup canola oil

2 large boneless skinless chicken breasts, cut into 2-inch chunks

2 large ripe Roma tomatoes, cut into quarters (optional)

½ cup water

3 tablespoons fish sauce

2 tablespoons sugar

Serves 2 to 4

- ■ **For the curry paste,** place the shallots, garlic and chili peppers in a food processor and process until smooth. Scrape the mixture into a small bowl. Add the shrimp paste and curry powder and mix well.
- ■ **For the chicken,** heat the oil in a wok over medium-high heat. Add ¼ cup of the curry paste and cook for 2 minutes, stirring constantly. The unused curry paste can be stored in the freezer for later use.
- ■ Add the chicken and tomatoes and mix well. Cook until bubbly, stirring often. Add the water, fish sauce and sugar and mix well. Simmer for 10 minutes or until the chicken is cooked through, stirring occasionally.

Note: This dish is traditionally made with a mortar and pestle, but a food processor works just as well.

This dish can be made with pork as well.

thai tidbit

The Thai currency is known as *baht*. Its value fluctuates daily, but currently it takes forty baht to equal one U.S. dollar.

This is definitely a great summer dessert that's elegant enough for grownups and friendly enough for kids. The beauty of this recipe is that it can be made entirely ahead of time, except for frying the ice cream, which needs to be done right before serving. The caramel sauce can be prepared two to three days earlier. You may purchase already-made caramel sauce, though it is not quite the same.

Fried Ice Cream Balls with Caramel Sauce

1 quart vanilla ice cream

3 eggs, beaten

1 teaspoon vanilla extract

1/2 teaspoon ground cinnamon

2 cups coconut flakes

2 cups corn flakes, coarsely crushed

Canola oil for frying

Caramel Sauce (page 67)

Serves 8

- Place 8 large scoops of ice cream on a sheet pan lined with waxed paper. Freeze the ice cream balls for 1 hour or until firm.
- Combine the eggs, vanilla and cinnamon in a bowl and mix well. Toss the coconut flakes and corn flakes in a bowl and mix well. Dip the ice cream balls into the egg mixture, and then into the coconut mixture, turning to coat evenly. Place the ice cream balls onto the sheet pan and freeze for 1 hour. Chill the remaining egg mixture.
- Remove the balls from the freezer and repeat the dipping procedure for a second coating. Return the balls to the sheet pan and freeze for 1 hour. Once the balls are frozen, they can be stored in a freezer-proof bag for one week or until ready to use.
- Heat the oil to 375 degrees in a heavy saucepan or deep fryer. Fry the ice cream balls, 2 at a time, until golden; drain on paper towels.
- Place the fried ice cream balls in individual dessert dishes and spoon the Caramel Sauce around the ice cream. Serve immediately.

thai tidbit

Thailand is twelve hours ahead of America's Central time zone; during daylight saving time, Thailand is thirteen hours ahead.

Caramel Sauce

2 cups sugar

1 cup (2 sticks) butter

1 cup half-and-half

3 tablespoons rum

Makes 2²/3 cups

- Sprinkle the sugar into a large cast-iron skillet. Cook over medium heat until the sugar melts and turns golden brown, stirring constantly. Remove from the heat.
- Add the butter and stir until melted.
- Return the mixture to the heat and add the half-and-half. Cook for 10 minutes, or until the mixture has thickened, stirring constantly.
- Stir in the rum; remove from the heat and let cool.
- Pour the sauce into a jar with a tight-fitting lid. Serve immediately, or keep in the refrigerator for 2 to 3 days. Reheat the sauce in a saucepan over gentle heat before serving, stirring occasionally.

noodles noodles

Crispy Noodles
Chiang Mai Noodles in Curry Sauce
Stir-Fried Broad Noodles with Garlicky Chicken and
  Collard Greens
Stir-Fried Noodles with Chicken and
  Mixed Vegetable Sauce

These noodles dishes are great for lunch because they are a quick one-dish meal. Most noodle dishes are easily found at any cafeteria or food center anywhere in Thailand. Chiang Mai noodles, on the other hand, can only be found in specialty restaurants or in the city of Chiang Mai.

Condiments always accompany noodle dishes in Thailand. These include sugar, fish sauce, vinegar, and chili flakes. Since the Thais like spicy food, the chili flakes are essential. The key to condiments is balance: we usually add them in a one-to-one ratio, except for chili flakes, which tend to tone down the other flavors. The noodle dishes can stand alone without the extra flavors of the condiments, but once you try it the Thai way, it is difficult to have it any other way!

One final note: most of the time Thais use a fork and a spoon simultaneously, but with noodle dishes, we use chopsticks. Happy eating!

Time-saving tips

Two days before
Make the Chiang Mai curry paste and refrigerate. Cut up the meat for all the dishes.

One day before
Prepare the Chiang Mai Curry Sauce.

Morning of the dinner
Prepare the Crispy Noodles.
Chop all the vegetables.

One hour before
Prepare the Broad Noodles with Garlicky Chicken and Collard Greens. Prepare the Stir-Fried Noodles with Chicken and Mixed Vegetable Sauce. Cut up the condiments for the Chiang Mai Noodles.

Who would have thought that a street snack such as mee-krob, which I never looked at twice in the market, would now catch my fancy? Crunchy, deep-fried rice vermicelli is cooked with a sweet and sour syrupy sauce. Sounds interesting, doesn't it? Eat it as a first course appetizer or as an afternoon snack.

Crispy Noodles

(mee-krob) | หมี่กรอบ

Canola oil for deep-frying

1 cup chopped dried thin rice noodles

2 tablespoons canola oil

1 garlic clove, chopped

1 shallot, chopped

1 cup shrimp, peeled and deveined

1 tablespoon white vinegar

1 tablespoon lime juice

1/2 cup (or 2 round disks) palm sugar

1/4 cup light soy sauce

3 tablespoons chopped cilantro

1 head pickled garlic, sliced (optional)

Serves 8 as an appetizer

- Heat the oil to 375 degrees in a deep saucepan or a deep fryer. Add the noodles in batches to the hot oil. Fry for a few seconds or until the noodles are puffy. Drain on paper towels and set aside.
- Heat 2 tablespoons of oil in a saucepan over medium-high heat. Add the garlic and shallot and stir-fry until the garlic is light golden brown. Chop the shrimp and add to the saucepan; stir-fry until the shrimp are pink. Add the vinegar, lime juice, palm sugar and soy sauce and mix well. Cook for 5 minutes or until bubbly.
- Remove from the heat and add the fried noodles. Stir until well combined. Garnish with cilantro and pickled garlic.

thai tidbit

It is not safe to drink the tap water in Thailand. Rainwater, a common water source, is collected from rooftops in large terra-cotta jars and then boiled.

My dear friend Myrt Davidson lived in Chiang Mai many years ago and fell in love with this dish. She requested that I include it in the cookbook, so here it is. It is made of noodles in a spicy curry sauce. Even though it's a bit complicated, I hope it becomes one of your favorites, too.

Chiang Mai Noodles in Curry Sauce

(kao-soi) ข้าวซอย

CURRY PASTE

¼ cup ground chili peppers

3 shallots, peeled and washed

2 teaspoons ground coriander, or
4 fresh coriander roots

1 teaspoon cumin

1 tablespoon curry powder

1 (1-inch) piece of galangal, sliced

½ teaspoon salt

CHIANG MAI NOODLES

2 (14-ounce) cans coconut milk

¼ cup Curry Paste (above)

1 pound beef or chicken, cut into 1-inch chunks

¼ cup fish sauce

3 tablespoons sugar

1 tablespoon black soy sauce

5 rounds dried Chinese egg noodles

Canola oil for deep-frying

2 tablespoons chopped cilantro

2 tablespoons chopped green onions

Serves 4

- *For the curry paste,* combine the chili peppers, shallots, coriander, cumin, curry powder, galangal and salt in a food processor. Process until a fine paste forms. Scrape the paste into a small bowl and set aside. This will make 1 cup of paste, but the recipe calls for only ¼ cup. You may freeze the remainder.
- *For the noodles,* heat the coconut milk in a wok over medium-high heat and bring to a boil. Reduce the heat and stir in ¼ cup of the Curry Paste; mix well. Add the beef, fish sauce, sugar and soy sauce and mix well. Simmer for 10 to 12 minutes or until the meat is cooked through, stirring occasionally.
- Cook 4 rounds of the noodles in boiling water in a medium-sized saucepan for 8 minutes or until tender. Drain and place the noodles in a serving bowl.
- Heat the oil to 375 degrees in a wok or a deep-fryer. Fry the remaining bundle of noodles in the hot oil until golden. Drain on paper towels and set aside for garnish.
- Pour the sauce over the boiled noodles and sprinkle with the cilantro, green onions and fried noodles.

Note: One 12-ounce package of noodles consists of 8 to 10 compressed rounds, though you will need only 5 of them. Cook 1 round of noodles per person, and fry 1 round for garnish.

Chiang Mai noodles are served with: fried shallots, fried dried chilies, lime wedges, and pickled cabbage.

Ah, another of my favorite things to order when I go home to Thailand. I prefer this dish with shrimp instead of chicken, though. You can order it with pork, beef, or any kind of shellfish. When I'm in Kansas, I long for this dish more because it is harder to find fresh noodles in my area. The noodles only last for a few days. If you can't find fresh noodles, you may also use Chinese egg noodles or thin rice noodles from Thai Kitchen.

Stir-Fried Broad Noodles with
Garlicky Chicken and Collard Greens

(pad-see-ew-gai)

1 cup sliced chicken breast

Pinch of white pepper

1 teaspoon soy sauce

6 to 8 ounces fresh flat broad rice noodles

2 tablespoons black soy sauce

1/4 cup canola oil

4 garlic cloves, chopped

1 tablespoon light soy sauce

1 tablespoon fish sauce

2 tablespoons sugar

3 eggs

2 cups sliced collard greens (baby collard greens preferred)

CONDIMENTS

Sugar

Fish sauce

White vinegar

Dried chili pepper flakes

Serves 2

- Place the chicken, pepper and soy sauce in a small bowl and mix well. Marinate for 10 minutes.
- Place the fresh noodles in a microwave-safe container. Microwave on medium-high for 2 minutes or until soft. If you are using dried noodles, soak them in water in a bowl for 15 minutes or until soft; drain. Add the black soy sauce to the noodles and mix well; set aside.
- Heat the wok over medium-high heat. Add the oil and garlic and stir-fry until the garlic is golden brown. Add the chicken and stir-fry until cooked through. Add the noodles and mix well.
- Stir in the light soy sauce, fish sauce and sugar and mix well. Stir-fry until well combined and push everything over to one side of the wok.
- Add the eggs and cook until lightly scrambled, stirring constantly. Stir in the collard greens and mix all of the ingredients together. Remove from the heat and serve with the condiments.

In Thailand, most noodle vendors will use only tender collard greens for this recipe. In the more formal restaurants (as opposed to the tables set up on the sidewalks) you will have a larger choice of vegetables. You can use Chinese egg noodles instead of the rice noodles in this recipe. Cook the noodles as directed, or deep fry them first, as many of the restaurants do. I avoid fried food as much as I can, so sautéing is enough.

Stir-Fried Noodles with Chicken and Mixed Vegetable Sauce

(gway-tio-rhad-na-gai)

ก๋วยเตี๋ยวราดหน้าไก่

NOODLES

6 to 8 ounces fresh flat broad rice noodles

2 tablespoons black soy sauce

2 tablespoons canola oil

2 garlic cloves, chopped

SAUCE

2 tablespoons canola oil

2 tablespoons minced garlic

2 cups thinly sliced chicken breasts

2 cups chopped mixed vegetables, such as carrots, cauliflower, collard greens and mushrooms

3 tablespoons light soy sauce

3 tablespoons oyster sauce

2 tablespoons sugar

6 cups Thai Stock (page 85) or water

1/4 cup cornstarch

1/2 cup water

Serves 2 to 4

- *For the noodles,* place the noodles in a microwave-safe container and microwave on Medium-High for 2 minutes or until soft. Cut the noodles into bite-size pieces and place in a bowl. Add the black soy sauce and mix well.
- Heat the oil in the wok until shimmering. Add the garlic and the noodles. Stir-fry for 5 minutes or until the noodles are soft. Remove the noodle mixture to a serving bowl and keep warm.
- *For the sauce,* heat the oil in the wok until shimmering. Add the garlic and stir-fry until golden. Add the chicken and stir-fry until cooked through. Add the vegetables and mix well. Stir in the light soy sauce, oyster sauce and sugar. Add the stock and bring the mixture to a boil.
- Combine the cornstarch and water in a small bowl and mix well. Add the cornstarch mixture to the wok and cook until thickened, stirring constantly. Serve the sauce over the noodles. Garnish with fried shallots, fried dried chilies, lime wedges and pickled cabbage.

noodles noodles

refreshingly low-fat

Grilled Beef Salad
Red Snapper Steamed
  in Lime Juice
Glass Noodle Soup
Savory Herbed Custard
Fresh Fruit Platter

Time-saving tips

Morning of the dinner
Grill the beef. Make the soup.
Chop the vegetables and herbs for
all the dishes. Peel all the fruit
without cutting.

Afternoon of the dinner
Cut the fruit and assemble on a
platter. Prepare and steam the herbed
custard. Finish the remainder of
the preparations.

I am very mindful of what I eat. Half of Thai food
I consider very low-fat and nutritious. This menu
is just that. You will find many other tasty, low-fat
choices in other chapters of this book as well.
Any kind of yum-Thai salad is virtually fat-free
(with the exception of meat).

Not only is this menu low-fat, but it is also
low-hassle. It is so simple that you do not have to
prepare any of the ingredients in advance.

This is a great way to use any leftover steak. But if you don't have any, start from scratch. By now you can already recognize the refreshing flavors of a Thai salad. Forget your ideas of bland diet food—this low-fat salad is full of zest, spice, lime, and mint.

Grilled Beef Salad

(yum-nua-yang)

ยำเนื้อย่าง

1 pound tender steak

1 small onion, thinly sliced lengthwise

1 cup grape tomatoes, halved

1 cucumber, thinly sliced crosswise

1/2 cup chopped cilantro

1/2 cup mint leaves, roughly chopped

1/2 cup chopped green onion

1/4 cup fish sauce

3 tablespoons lime juice

1/2 tablespoon sugar

1 to 2 tablespoons crushed Thai peppers or cayenne peppers (optional)

Serves 2 to 4

- Grill the beef over hot coals until cooked to the desired degree of doneness. Do not overcook; it should still be slightly pink in the center. Let rest for 10 minutes and slice thinly.
- Combine the beef, onion, tomatoes, cucumber, cilantro, mint and green onion in a large bowl and mix well. Combine the fish sauce, lime juice, sugar and peppers in a small bowl and mix well.
- Add the fish sauce mixture to the beef mixture and toss to combine.

refreshingly low-fat

thai tidbit

Most schools teach English beginning in the fifth grade, and it is a required class until the student graduates. Some private schools start earlier.

I was blessed to grow up by the sea and I learned to love fish at an early age. This recipe will appeal to all cultures, whether you grew up near a beach or not. It produces a mild but zesty fish which will quickly become one of your new-found favorites. It is a well-known dish from my hometown, Prachuabkirikhan. It's a meal we can eat at a restaurant on the beach.

Red Snapper Steamed in Lime Juice

(pla-nung-ma-nao)

ปลา นึ่ง มะนาว

1 whole red snapper, scaled and washed, or
2 red snapper fillets

3 garlic cloves, minced

1¹/2 tablespoons fish sauce

1¹/2 tablespoons lime juice

3 tablespoons Thai Stock (page 85) or water

¹/4 cup chopped cilantro

Serves 2

- Place the fish on a large oven-proof platter. Combine the garlic, fish sauce, lime juice and stock in a bowl and mix well. Pour the mixture over the fish.
- Place the platter in a bamboo or metal steamer and steam for 10 minutes on medium-high heat, or until the fish is opaque and flakes easily.
- If you do not have a steamer, you may bake the fish at 350 degrees for 15 minutes or until the fish is opaque and flakes easily. Sprinkle with the cilantro before serving.

thai tidbit

The floating market is a popular tourist site near Bangkok. It is comprised of boats filled with fruits and vegetables floating on the water.

This is a dish that you won't normally find in a restaurant, but it's a staple recipe in Thai homes or school cafeterias. We eat it at least once a week. I often eat it as a meal by itself, but I usually add the noodle condiments. When I think of a Thai comfort food, this dish comes to mind. It's also commonly used for the treatment of head colds.

Glass Noodle Soup

(gaeng-jud-woon-sen)   แกงจืดวุ้นเส้น

1 pound ground pork

3 garlic cloves, finely minced

1/2 teaspoon white pepper

2 cilantro roots, chopped, or 1/2 teaspoon coriander powder

2 tablespoons light soy sauce

10 cups Thai Stock (page 85)

1 (2-ounce) individual bundle of glass noodles

1 cucumber, cut diagonally into slices 1/4-inch thick

1 (12-ounce) package silken tofu

1/4 cup plus 1 tablespoon fish sauce

1/2 bunch green onions, cut into 2-inch pieces

1/4 cup chopped cilantro

Serves 6

- Combine the pork, garlic, pepper, cilantro roots and soy sauce in a bowl and mix well. Shape the pork mixture into 1-inch balls (you may freeze at this point).
- Bring the stock to a boil in a large saucepan over high heat. Add the pork balls and cook for 10 minutes or until cooked through. Add the glass noodles and mix well.
- Reduce the heat to a simmer and add the cucumber and tofu. Cook for 5 minutes or until the glass noodles become translucent. Add the fish sauce and green onions and mix well. Remove from the heat. Sprinkle with the cilantro and serve.

thai tidbit

Since you kick your opponent, no shoes are worn during Thai kick-boxing.

This is my sister's signature dish. It's her claim to fame at our house since she doesn't cook that often. This is another of my regulars when I return home. Typically, this custard is eaten with gaeng som, a spicy soup-like curry at a school cafeteria. Even though I now eat it without the curry, it still reminds me of how I used to eat it growing up.

Savory Herbed Custard

(kai-dtun)   ไข่ตุ๋น

3 eggs, beaten

1 cup water

1 tablespoon soy sauce

Pinch of pepper

1 tablespoon chopped cilantro

1 tablespoon chopped chives or green onion

Serves 2

- Combine the eggs, water, soy sauce, pepper, cilantro and chives in a bowl and mix well. Pour the egg mixture into an oven-proof bowl or a 4-inch ramekin.
- Place in a steamer and steam for 10 minutes on medium-high heat or until a knife inserted in the center comes out clean.

Any combination of tropical fruits will work. Here is a sample list of what I usually serve.

Fresh Fruit Platter

(pol-a-my)   ผลไม้

1 pineapple, sliced

2 mangoes, sliced

1 ripe papaya, sliced

1 pint strawberries

1 bunch grapes

4 kiwifruit, sliced

1 star fruit, sliced

Mint for garnish

Serves 2 to 4

- Arrange the fruits artfully on a platter and garnish with mint.

Note: Some tropical fruits are a bit difficult to cut. For the pineapple, cut using a 6-inch boning knife or a chef's knife. Cut each end off. Place the remaining pineapple cut end down on a cutting board. Carefully remove the skin with the knife by cutting around the pineapple in long, vertical cuts. Remove the "eyes" with a small paring knife. Wash the skinned pineapple and cut into quarters. Cut away the core and slice into small triangles. For instructions on cutting mangoes, refer to the note on page 27. For the papaya, cut in half, scoop out the black seeds with a spoon and peel off the skin. Cut each half horizontally into 4 or 5 small slices.

everyday home cooking

Menu for 4 to 6 people

Ginger Beef
Garlic Pepper Pork
Stuffed Omelet
Omelet with Pork
Thai Stock
Dipping Sauces
Curry Pastes

These dishes are definitely everyday home-cooked meals. They are great for breakfast, lunch, or supper. You'll notice that we eat a lot of eggs. If you have ever visited Thailand, you will know that instead of table salt, we use naam-pla-prik, a fish sauce with chili peppers and sometimes a squeeze of lime juice. But for most meals, it's just fish sauce and peppers.

Time-saving tips

One day before
Make the filling for the Stuffed Omelet.
Cut up the meat for all the dishes.
Make the Thai Stock.

Morning of the dinner
Chop the vegetables.

Thirty minutes before dinner
Prepare the Garlic Pepper Pork,
Ginger Beef, and Omelet with Pork.
Assemble the Stuffed Omelet.

Ginger is supposed to be good for your digestive system. At least that's what I heard from my mom when I was young. It turned out to be true. Ginger serves as an antinausea remedy. Even though it is not spicy, this dish still has plenty of heat due to this root vegetable. You may also make this dish with chicken.

Ginger Beef

(pat-king-nua)   ผัดขิงเนื้อ

2 cups sliced beef sirloin

1 teaspoon soy sauce

1 teaspoon sugar

Pinch of white pepper

3 tablespoons canola oil

1/2 cup thinly sliced ginger

1 tablespoon oyster sauce

2 tablespoons light soy sauce

1 tablespoon sugar

1/2 cup Thai Stock (page 85) or water

1 to 4 fresh red jalapeño peppers, cut into long thin strips

1/2 wood ear mushroom, thinly sliced

3 green onions, cut into 2-inch pieces

Serves 2 to 4

- Combine the beef, 1 teaspoon soy sauce, 1 teaspoon sugar and the pepper in a bowl and mix well; set aside.
- Heat the oil in a wok over medium-high heat until shimmering. Add the ginger and stir-fry until golden brown. Add the beef and stir-fry until cooked to the desired degree of doneness.
- Stir in the oyster sauce, 2 tablespoons light soy sauce, 1 tablespoon sugar, the stock, jalapeño peppers and mushroom and mix well. Add the green onions and toss to combine.

Note: Look for a wood ear mushroom in dried form. It is sold either whole or pre-sliced and is a dark brown in color. It has a chewy texture and an earthy flavor like most mushrooms. Soak the mushroom in warm water to reconstitute.

thai tidbit

Grocery stores are not common outside of Bangkok. In most towns, people congregate every morning at the fresh market downtown.

This is a common breakfast for Thai students. Of course, you can eat it at any meal. This simple dish is very garlicky, so be sure to brush, floss and rinse your mouth well. Otherwise, you'll end up with garlic breath for the day!

Garlic Pepper Pork

(mu-tot-gra-tiam-prik-thai)

หมูทอดกระเทียมพริกไทย

½ head garlic, minced

1 teaspoon white pepper

1½ tablespoons light soy sauce

2 tablespoons water

1½ tablespoons fish sauce

1 teaspoon black soy sauce

1 tablespoon sugar

1 pound pork, thinly sliced

¼ cup canola oil

Cucumber slices

Sriracha sauce

Serves 2 to 4

- Combine the garlic, pepper, light soy sauce, water, fish sauce, black soy sauce and sugar in a large bowl and mix well. Add the pork and stir to combine. Marinate for 15 minutes.
- Heat the oil in a wok over medium-high heat until shimmering. Drain the pork, discarding the marinade. Add the pork to the wok and stir fry until cooked through.
- Serve with cucumber slices and Sriracha sauce, if desired.

Note: This dish can also be made with beef, chicken, shrimp or calamari.

everyday home cooking

thai tidbit

Thai names are quite long. Everyone has an official first name that is used by teachers and government officials, but people also have a one-syllable nickname that is used among friends. There are no middle names in Thailand.

An elegant way to serve eggs, this is suitable for both breakfast and supper.

Stuffed Omelet

(kai-jio-yat-sai)

ไข่ยัดไส้

FILLING

½ tablespoon canola oil

½ onion, chopped

½ cup ground pork

½ cup chopped tomato

1 tablespoon fish sauce

Pinch of white pepper

Pinch of sugar

2 tablespoons chopped green onions

OMELET

6 eggs

2 teaspoons soy sauce

3 tablespoons canola oil

Sriracha sauce

Cucumber slices

Serves 2 to 4

- *For the filling,* heat the oil in a wok over medium-high heat until shimmering. Add the onion and stir-fry until translucent. Add the pork and stir-fry until cooked through. Add the tomato, fish sauce, pepper, sugar and green onions and mix well; set aside.
- *For the omelet,* combine the eggs and soy sauce in a bowl and whisk until frothy.
- Heat the oil in a wok or a skillet over medium-high heat until shimmering. Add the egg mixture to the wok. Swirl the wok to evenly coat the bottom with the egg mixture. Lift one corner of the eggs as they begin to set to allow the remaining egg mixture to cook.
- Spoon the filling over the omelet and fold into a square. Flip the omelet onto a serving plate. Serve with Sriracha sauce and cucumber slices.

thai tidbit

People drive on the left side of the road in Thailand, and the metric system is used for measurements.

This egg dish is one of my favorite breakfast dishes. Because I grew up in Thailand, I still like savory, salty things for breakfast. Thais consider sweet things such as cereal as a dessert rather than a starter. The omelet produces a crusty outer coating with a soft, moist inside. It's hard to beat! (No pun intended!)

Omelet with Pork

(kai-jio-mu-sop)   ไข่เจียวหมูสับ

4 eggs, beaten

1/2 cup ground pork

2 tablespoons chopped green onions

1 tablespoon light soy sauce

Pinch of sugar

Pinch of white pepper

1/4 cup canola oil

Sriracha sauce

Serves 2

- Combine the eggs, pork, green onions, soy sauce, sugar and pepper in a bowl and mix well.
- Heat the oil in a wok or an 8-inch omelet skillet over medium-high heat. Add the egg mixture to the wok. Swirl the wok to evenly coat the bottom with the egg mixture. Lift one corner of the eggs as they begin to set to allow the remaining egg mixture to cook.
- Cook for 10 minutes or until firm and golden. Flip the omelet with a large spatula. Reduce the heat to medium-low and cook for 10 minutes or until golden on both sides.
- Serve with Sriracha sauce.

Thai Stock

(naam-soup)   น้ำซุป

1 package pork neck bones (or any meat bones)

10 white peppercorns

1 onion, cut into quarters

1/2 cup coarsely chopped cilantro

1/4 cup light soy sauce

8 cups water

Makes 8 cups

- Combine the pork bones, peppercorns, onion, cilantro, soy sauce and water in a large saucepan and bring to a boil over medium-high heat.
- Simmer for 30 minutes.
- Strain the liquid into a separate container and skim off the fat. Refrigerate for up to 2 weeks or freeze in ice cube trays. Once frozen, you may remove the cubes to a freezer-proof plastic bag.

Note: This is a key ingredient in many Thai recipes. Make a large batch and freeze the remainder. Freezing stock in ice-cube trays is especially convenient when you need just a few tablespoons of stock in a recipe.

Serve this spicy sauce with any main dish. It is the equivalent of table salt in Thailand.

Fish Sauce with Chili Peppers

(naam-plah-prik) | น้ำปลาพริก

2 tablespoons fish sauce

2 chili peppers, finely chopped

Makes 2 tablespoons

- Combine the fish sauce and chili peppers in a small bowl and mix well.

This sauce will forever change your way of eating bland boiled eggs. It's tart, sweet, and salty all at once. And it's good on meat, too—especially grilled meat.

Sauce for Boiled Eggs

(naam-jim-kai-dtom) | น้ำจิ้มไข่ต้ม

2 tablespoons fish sauce

1 tablespoon lime juice

1 tablespoon palm sugar

1 large shallot, sliced

1 to 2 Thai peppers or cayenne chili peppers

Makes 1/4 cup

- Combine the fish sauce, lime juice and palm sugar in a bowl and stir until the sugar has dissolved.
- Stir in the shallot and peppers.
- Remove to a condiment bowl and serve.

thai tidbit

Bangkok means "The City of Angels."

Curry paste is the secret of all Thai curries. It is the most labor intensive of any kitchen task. Most Thai homes buy ready-made paste at the fresh market. My mom lovingly spends a good hour making her own. She uses the modern technology of a food processor to speed things up, but with old-world technique to create the smooth thick paste. That's why her curries surpass all others. I know how arduous this work is, so with each bite I truly appreciate all the care she takes.

Red Curry Paste

(naam-prik-gaeng-phet)

น้ำพริกแกงเผ็ด

3 stalks fresh lemongrass

3 fresh galangal roots

Zest of 1 Kaffir lime

2 heads garlic

10 to 20 dried Thai chili peppers

1 teaspoon salt

1 tablespoon shrimp paste

Makes 1 to 1 1/4 cups

- Chop the lemongrass and galangal into small pieces.
- Combine the lemongrass, galangal, lime zest, garlic, chili peppers, salt and shrimp paste in a food processor and process until a smooth paste forms.

Note: This is the base curry paste recipe for all the other curry paste variations. Refer to this recipe when making the other curry paste recipes. Curry paste can be stored in the refrigerator for up to 2 weeks or frozen for up to 3 months.

Panang Curry Paste

(naam-prik-gaeng-panang)

น้ำพริกแกงพะแนง

1 recipe Red Curry Paste (above)

1/2 teaspoon cinnamon

1/2 teaspoon nutmeg

2 star anise

1 white cardamom seed

1 tablespoon coriander seeds

Makes 1 to 1 1/4 cups

- Prepare the Red Curry Paste, adding 1/2 teaspoon cinnamon, 1/2 teaspoon nutmeg, 2 star anise, 1 white cardamom seed and 1 tablespoon coriander seeds. Place all of the ingredients in a food processor and process until smooth.

I was tempted not to include these recipes in the book, since nowadays most people use prepared curry paste. I myself use store-bought paste. But I want to share with you how true Thai curry paste is made. If you want to try to make it at home, I want you to have the authentic recipe, not an adapted one that doesn't resemble Thai curries. After all that talk, feel free to purchase a reliable curry paste from a good source such as Thai Kitchen. They really are authentic and well-made.

Yellow Curry Paste

(naam-prik-gaeng-gah-ri)　　น้ำพริกแกงกะหรี่

1 recipe Red Curry Paste (page 87)

2 tablespoons curry powder

Makes 1 to 1 1/4 cups

- Prepare the Red Curry Paste, adding 2 tablespoons of curry powder. Place all of the ingredients in a food processor and process until smooth.

Green Curry Paste

(naam-prik-gaeng-kio-wan)

น้ำพริกแกงเขียวหวาน

1 recipe Red Curry Paste (page 87)

10 to 20 fresh green chili peppers

Makes 1 to 1 1/4 cups

- Prepare the Red Curry Paste, substituting the fresh green chili peppers for the dried chili peppers. Place all of the ingredients in a food processor and process until smooth.

Mussamun Curry Paste

(naam-prik-gaeng-mussamun)

น้ำพริกแกงมัสมั่น

1 recipe Panang Curry Paste (page 87)

1 teaspoon black peppercorns

1 teaspoon caraway seeds

Makes 1 to 1 1/4 cups

- Prepare the Panang Curry Paste, adding 1 teaspoon of black peppercorns and 1 teaspoon of caraway seeds. Place all of the ingredients in a food processor and process until smooth.

thai tidbit

When Thai people peel vegetables or cut fruit, they direct the knife outward away from their bodies.

street snacks

À la carte menu

Curry Puffs	Steamed Pork Dumplings
Shrimp Toast	Fried Bananas
Dried Thai Beef	Iced Coffee
Fried Won Tons	

Time-saving tips

One month before
Make the Curry Puffs (without baking) and freeze. Make the Shrimp Toast (without frying) and freeze. Make the won tons (without frying) and freeze. Make the pork dumplings (without steaming) and freeze. Season the beef for the dried beef and freeze.

Two hours before
Thaw out the Curry Puffs at room temperature for thirty minutes and bake.

One hour before
Steam the pork dumplings.
Make the batter for the Fried Bananas.

Thirty minutes before
Fry the dried beef, the won tons, and the Shrimp Toast. Using new oil, fry the bananas.

Every town in Thailand has a fresh market called the tha-laad. There, you can find all the treats included in this chapter. These are the childhood foods I grew up eating. Now you can find an array of snacks at the evening market. The fresh market is open every day all day (with the freshest items found in the morning) and provides the essential food for cooking that day. The evening market (tha-laad-nudt) is usually open twice a week if not more; it varies from town to town. It includes an impromptu restaurant and has a greater focus on clothing and other nonfood items. It has the atmosphere of an American county fair. These recipes can serve as a snack or as an appetizer.

This is a treat that always reminds me of traveling by train. At each station you'll hear vendors trying to sell curry puffs while the train idles briefly between towns. Today curry puffs are sold at upscale bakeries throughout the country. You'll love the rich curry flavor from the filling and the flakiness of the pastry.

Curry Puffs

(ka-ri-puff)

กะหรี่ปั๊บ

2 tablespoons canola oil

2 garlic cloves, chopped

1/2 cup chopped onion

1 cup ground chicken breast

2 tablespoons curry powder

1 tablespoon sugar

1 teaspoon salt

1 tablespoon soy sauce

1/2 teaspoon white pepper

1 1/2 cups potato cubes, parboiled

1 sheet puff pastry

1 egg yolk, beaten

Makes 18 curry puff appetizers

- Heat the oil in a wok over medium-high heat until shimmering. Add the garlic and onion and stir-fry until golden brown. Add the chicken, curry powder, sugar, salt, soy sauce and pepper and mix well. Stir-fry until the chicken is cooked through. Add the potatoes and stir-fry for 2 minutes. Remove from the heat and let cool slightly.
- Thaw the puff pastry using the package directions. Roll the pastry into an 11×11-inch square. Cut the square vertically into thirds. Cut the vertical pieces horizontally into thirds, making 9 small squares.
- Place 1 tablespoon of the filling in the center of each pastry square. Brush the edges of the pastry squares with the egg yolk and fold to form a triangle. Pinch the edges together to seal each triangle. Place the curry puffs on a baking sheet and refrigerate for 30 minutes.
- Bake at 425 degrees for 15 to 20 minutes, or until golden brown. Serve with Cucumber Relish (page 15). Though they are scrumptious on their own, it's more refreshing to enjoy the hot, crisp pastries with the cool Cucumber Relish.

Note: You will have leftover filling that you can freeze or use with another box of puff pastry.

Traditionally, this toast is made with ground pork. Shrimp, being costly, are reserved for special occasions. Once you bite into this crunchy fried snack dipped in sweet sauce, you will overlook its "non-low-fat status." Have plenty of napkins ready, as you will want to eat more than one!

Shrimp Toast

(kha-nom-pang-naa-gung)

ขนมปังหน้ากุ้ง

1 pound cooked shrimp with tails removed, peeled and deveined

3 cilantro roots, or 1/2 teaspoon coriander powder

2 tablespoons chopped cilantro

3 garlic cloves, peeled

1/2 teaspoon freshly ground white pepper

2 tablespoons light soy sauce

1 teaspoon sugar

20 stale slices of firm white bread, crusts removed, cut into 2 or 4 triangles

3 to 4 cups canola oil for deep-frying

Makes 40 large toasts or 80 small toasts

- Place the shrimp, cilantro roots, cilantro, garlic, white pepper, soy sauce and sugar in a food processor and process until smooth. Spread the shrimp mixture in a thin, even layer on each slice of bread.
- Heat the oil to 375 degrees in a large, heavy skillet or deep fryer. Working in batches, fry the toasts shrimp-side down until golden. The toasts will float when they are done. Turn the toasts over and fry for 1 to 2 minutes longer.
- Drain on paper towels and arrange on a platter. Serve with Spring Roll Sauce (page 13).

Note: You may assemble the shrimp toasts up until the point of frying and freeze them. Arrange in a single layer on a baking sheet and freeze. Once frozen, they can be placed together in a freezer-proof plastic bag. Thaw them out before frying. Be forewarned: your freezer will smell like shrimp until you put them in a freezer bag.

Dried Thai Beef

(nua-kem)

เนื้อเค็ม

1 pound beef sirloin, cut into 6 to 8 pieces

1 teaspoon salt

1 teaspoon fish sauce

Canola oil for frying

Serves 6

- Combine the beef, salt and fish sauce in a bowl and mix well.
- If the climate allows, air-dry the beef in the sun for a day. Keep the meat covered with fine-mesh. If you prefer, you may refrigerate the beef overnight.
- Heat the oil to 375 degrees in a wok over medium-high heat. Fry the beef for 5 minutes or until crispy. Drain on paper towels and serve with sticky rice.

This crunchy appetizer is similar to spring rolls, but with fewer ingredients.

Fried Won Tons

(krew-krub) เกี๊ยวกรอบ

2 garlic cloves, minced

1 coriander root, mashed, or 1/4 teaspoon coriander powder

1 cup ground pork

1 teaspoon white pepper

2 teaspoons soy sauce

1 teaspoon sugar

1 tablespoon chopped cilantro

1 tablespoon chopped green onion

1 egg yolk, beaten

1/2 (60- to 80-count) package small won ton wrappers

1 tablespoon canola oil

Canola oil for deep-frying

Makes 25 to 30 wontons

- Combine the garlic and the coriander root in a small bowl and mix into a paste.
- Heat a wok over medium-high heat. Add the garlic paste and stir-fry until golden brown. Add the pork and stir-fry until cooked through. Add the pepper, soy sauce and sugar and mix well. Remove from the heat. Stir in the cilantro and green onion.
- Lay 1 won ton wrapper on a smooth flat work surface. Cover the remaining wrappers with moist paper towels. Place 1 tablespoon of the pork mixture in the center of the wrapper. Moisten the edges with the egg yolk and fold to form a triangle. Repeat the procedure until all of the pork mixture is used.
- Heat the oil to 375 degrees in a large, heavy-bottomed saucepan or deep fryer. Fry the won tons until golden and drain on paper towels. Serve with Spring Roll Sauce (page 13).

Note: Since pork is usually sold in 1-pound packages, you will have to double the recipe to use the entire package. If you want to plan ahead, this dish freezes well. Arrange a single layer of won tons on a baking sheet and freeze. Once individually frozen, store the won tons together in a freezer-proof plastic bag for up to 3 months. Thaw before frying.

This is one of China's best contributions to Thai cuisine. It is a must for me every time I go home. It is a great appetizer with a mellow filling and slightly chewy dough. Serve with soy dipping sauce and Sriracha sauce.

Steamed Pork Dumplings

(ka-nom-jeeb) ขนมจีบ

1 pound ground pork

2 garlic cloves, finely minced

¼ cup chopped cilantro

2 tablespoons light soy sauce

½ teaspoon white pepper

½ tablespoon sugar

2 tablespoons cornstarch

1 egg

¼ cup water

1 (60- to 80-count) package round won ton wrappers

Makes 40 dumplings

- Combine the pork, garlic, cilantro, soy sauce, pepper, sugar, cornstarch, egg and water in a food processor and process until smooth. (If you don't have a food processor, you may combine the ingredients in a bowl by hand.)
- Lay 1 won ton wrapper on a smooth flat surface. Cover the remaining wrappers with moist paper towels. Place 1 tablespoon of the pork mixture in the center of the wrapper. Pull the sides of the wrapper toward the center, shaping it into a cup. Pleat the edges by overlapping and pinching the wrapper together. Leave the pork visible in the middle. Repeat the procedure until all of the pork mixture has been used.
- Place a single layer of dumplings in a lightly oiled bamboo or metal steamer. Steam for 10 to 12 minutes over medium-high heat, or until the pork mixture is cooked through. Remove and serve with Soy Dipping Sauce (below).

Soy Dipping Sauce

¼ cup soy sauce

1 tablespoon sugar

1 tablespoon white wine vinegar

1 green onion, finely chopped

Makes ¼ cup

- Combine the soy sauce, sugar, vinegar and green onion in a bowl and mix well. Serve in a condiment bowl with the dumplings.

Think of this as banana fritters. I didn't appreciate this dish in Thailand because it is so widely available. It's on every corner of every town. This version has more crunch, body, and puffiness than the original batter. I prefer serving it with honey or maple syrup, whereas the Thais eat it plain.

Fried Bananas

(glauy-todd or glauy-kaek)

กล้วยทอด - กล้วยแขก

1 cup rice flour

6 tablespoons cornstarch

2 teaspoons baking powder

1/2 cup shredded unsweetened coconut

1/2 teaspoon salt

2 tablespoons sugar

1 tablespoon toasted sesame seeds

1 1/2 cups water

Canola oil for deep-frying

4 green bananas,
sliced 1/4-inch-thick lengthwise

Serves 4 to 6

- Combine the flour, cornstarch, baking powder, shredded coconut, salt, sugar and sesame seeds in a bowl and mix well. Add the water and stir until well combined.
- Heat the oil to 375 degrees in a large heavy-bottomed saucepan or deep-fryer. Dip the banana slices into the batter and gently drop into the hot oil. Fry until the slices are golden brown and float to the surface, turning once. Drain on paper towels.
- Serve drizzled with or dipped in honey or maple syrup, if desired.

Note: If you have an oriental grocery store near you, look for medium-sized Manzano bananas. They have a unique sweet flavor, with just a hint of cinnamon.

This is the richest, creamiest coffee that I have ever tasted. I once drank all 16 ounces of this coffee in one big gulp. It gave me an instant brain freeze and headache. I won't do that again! It is best when savored slowly. My brother is a coffee connoisseur and manages a coffee shop; this is his treat to me when I go home. After experimenting with different types of coffees in this recipe, I find that instant coffee (such as Nescafé) works best.

Iced Coffee

(ga-gae-yen)

กาแฟเย็น

2 cups freshly brewed very strong coffee, still hot

2 tablespoons sweetened condensed milk

Serves 1 to 2

- Combine the coffee and condensed milk in a small pitcher and mix well. Pour into tall glasses filled with ice. Delicious!

more desserts, please!

White Chocolate Raspberry Cheesecake
White Chocolate Shortcakes with
  Caramelized Bananas
White Chocolate Crème Brûlée
Coconut Cake with Cream Cheese Icing
Lime Curd Tart with Tropical Fruits
Key Lime Coconut Bars

I know, I know!! This is not your typical Thai fare. But these desserts are full of tropical flavors that complement Thai food perfectly. For years they've been my favorite desserts to serve. Who doesn't love dessert? These grand finales all have an exotic twist, yet they are not complicated to make. In fact, a lot of them are quick and easy. Plan ahead, as a few of these can be made and frozen easily. I'm dedicating this chapter to our dear Texan friend Tim Bennett, who enjoys sweets—not just sticky rice and mangoes, but other kinds as well.

Time-saving tips

One month before
Make the crust for the Lime Curd Tart; press on the tart pan and freeze. Make the crust for the Key Lime Coconut Bars; press in the pan and freeze. Thaw both crusts before baking.

One week before
Prepare and bake the coconut cake and freeze. Make the cream cheese icing and refrigerate. Make the lime curd and refrigerate. Make the raspberry sauce and refrigerate.

One day before
Assemble the coconut cake and refrigerate. Make the Key Lime Coconut Bars and refrigerate. Make the White Chocolate Crème Brûlée and refrigerate.

Day of the party
Bake the crust for the tart and cut up fruit for the tart; assemble and chill. Bake the White Chocolate Shortcakes.

Just before the party
Make the banana sauce for the shortcakes.

I don't know very many people who don't like cheesecake. How can one resist this sweet cream cake topped with tart raspberry sauce? You can indulge in this grand finale all year round, even without fresh raspberries—frozen ones will work just fine. The red color makes this dessert especially appropriate on Valentine's Day, Fourth of July, and Christmas.

White Chocolate Raspberry Cheesecake

CRUST

3/4 cup graham cracker crumbs

1/2 cup sliced almonds, toasted and finely chopped

3 tablespoons butter, melted

1/4 cup sugar

FILLING

6 ounces white chocolate, chopped

24 ounces cream cheese, softened

1/2 cup sugar

1 egg yolk

3 eggs

4 teaspoons all-purpose flour

1 teaspoon vanilla extract

1 pint fresh raspberries

- *For the crust,* combine the graham cracker crumbs, almonds, butter and sugar in a bowl and mix well.
- Press the crumb mixture over the bottom and up the side of a 9-inch springform pan.
- *For the filling,* place the white chocolate in a metal bowl set over a pan of barely simmering water. Melt the chocolate, stirring until smooth. Remove from the heat and let cool slightly.
- Beat the cream cheese in a large mixing bowl until light and fluffy. Add the sugar and beat until smooth.
- Add the egg yolk and the eggs, one at a time, beating well after each addition.
- Add the flour, vanilla and white chocolate and beat until smooth.
- Scatter the raspberries over the crust and pour the filling into the crust. Tap the pan on the counter a few times to remove any air bubbles.
- Bake at 350 degrees for 15 minutes. Reduce the heat to 225 degrees and bake for 1 hour and 10 minutes, or until the top is firm. Turn off the heat and remove the cheesecake. Run a knife around the edge of the cheesecake and return it to the oven. Leave the oven door open slightly and let the cheesecake cool completely.
- Remove the cheesecake from the oven and cover loosely with plastic wrap. Chill for 1 day or longer before serving. If you are making this in advance, remove the side of the pan and freeze. Once frozen, wrap tightly with plastic wrap and foil. This cheesecake may be frozen for up to 3 months. Thaw overnight before serving.

RASPBERRY SAUCE

1 (12-ounce) package frozen
raspberries, thawed

3 tablespoons sugar

3 tablespoons orange juice

1/2 cup water

Serves 12

■ *For the raspberry sauce,* combine the raspberries, sugar, orange juice and water in a saucepan and mix well. Bring to a boil over medium-high heat. Reduce the heat to low and cook for 10 minutes, stirring often. Remove from the heat and let cool slightly. Strain the raspberry mixture through a sieve into a glass jar with a tight-fitting lid, discarding the seeds. Store the sauce in the tightly sealed jar and refrigerate for up to 2 weeks.

■ To serve, place a slice of cheesecake onto a dessert plate and drizzle with raspberry sauce. Garnish with a mint sprig and fresh raspberries.

thai tidbit

A popular sport in Thailand, Indonesia, and Malaysia is "ta-graw." The game involves kicking a woven rattan ball over a net.

The inspiration for this dessert was a scone recipe. I wanted something warm, easy, and unique for a winter dessert, so I came up with this recipe. The shortcake is very tender, and thanks to the sour cream, it doesn't dry out quickly. I pair the shortcake with caramelized bananas, an acknowledgment to bananas Foster.

White Chocolate Shortcakes with Caramelized Bananas

more desserts, please

102

SHORTCAKES

2 cups all-purpose flour

1/2 cup sugar

1 tablespoon baking powder

1/4 teaspoon salt

1/2 cup (1 stick) butter, cut into small pieces

1 cup sour cream

6 ounces white chocolate, finely chopped

Milk for brushing

CARAMELIZED BANANAS

4 very ripe bananas

1/3 cup butter

2/3 cup packed brown sugar

Pinch of salt

2 tablespoons rum

2 tablespoons crème de banana

Vanilla ice cream or whipped cream

Serves 4 (with extra shortcakes)

- *For the shortcakes,* combine the flour, sugar, baking powder and salt in a bowl and mix well. Cut the butter into the flour mixture until it resembles course crumbs. Stir in the sour cream and mix well. Add the white chocolate and stir until combined. The dough will be thick.
- Place the dough onto a lightly floured surface and shape into two 6-inch rounds. Cut each round into 4 triangles. The dough can be frozen at this point. Thaw out at room temperature for 15 minutes before baking. Place the dough triangles on a baking sheet and brush lightly with milk. Bake for 9 to 11 minutes, or until golden brown.
- *For the caramelized bananas,* peel and cut the bananas into 1-inch chunks and set aside.
- Melt the butter in a medium saucepan over medium-high heat. Add the sugar and salt and cook until bubbly, stirring constantly. Sir in the bananas and cook until soft. Pour in the rum and crème de banana and mix well. Cook for 2 to 3 minutes, stirring frequently, and remove from the heat.
- *To assemble,* place 1 shortcake on each dessert plate. Pour the banana sauce over the shortcake. Place 1 large scoop of vanilla ice cream or whipped cream on top and serve.

Note: You can freeze the shortcake dough for up to 3 months.

Every time I make a white wedding cake or an angel food cake, I end up with plenty of leftover egg yolks. I don't like throwing things away, so crème brûlée is the best choice. You can make it a couple of days ahead and chill it. I find that if I broil the surface right before serving, the filling is too warm. I prefer it entirely chilled, so I broil it about two hours earlier and chill it. This will give a shiny crunchy crust with a cool and creamy filling.

White Chocolate Crème Brûlée

CRÈME BRÛLÉE

1¹/₂ cups heavy cream or whipping cream

¹/₂ cup milk

4 ounces white chocolate, chopped

¹/₂ cup granulated sugar

8 egg yolks

Pinch of salt

1 teaspoon vanilla extract

SPRINKLING SUGAR

2 tablespoons granulated sugar

2 tablespoons Demerara sugar or light brown sugar

Makes 6 to 8 custards

- *For the crème brûlée,* heat the cream and milk in a saucepan over low heat. Add the white chocolate and cook until melted, stirring constantly.
- Add the sugar and stir until dissolved. Remove from the heat.
- Whisk the egg yolks, salt and vanilla in a mixing bowl until well blended.
- Add the white chocolate mixture to the egg yolk mixture gradually, whisking constantly. Pour slowly so the hot cream does not curdle the yolks. Strain the mixture through a fine-mesh sieve into a bowl.
- Carefully ladle the mixture into 6 to 8 custard cups or ramekins. Place the cups in a 9×13-inch glass pan. Carefully pour boiling water into the pan until it reaches halfway up the sides of the cups. Bake for 45 to 55 minutes, or until the surface is set and the centers still jiggle slightly. Remove from the oven and let cool to room temperature in the pan of water.
- Remove the ramekins from the water and chill, covered, in the refrigerator.
- *For the sprinkling sugar,* combine the granulated sugar and the Demerara sugar in a small bowl and mix well. Sprinkle 1¹/₂ teaspoons of the sugar mixture onto each cup. Broil 3 inches from the heat source for 1 minute or until golden brown. Keep a close watch so the custards don't burn.

I love coconut. I will eat anything that has coconut as an ingredient. I've sampled many versions of coconut cakes and most have boiled icings, which I find to be too billowy sweet. I found my solution by substituting melt-in-your-mouth cream cheese icing. Among the varieties of desserts I make, this moist yet fluffy cake always receives rave reviews. And you would not believe that I used a store-bought cake mix!

Coconut Cake with Cream Cheese Icing

CAKE

1 (2-layer) white cake mix

1 (14-ounce) can coconut milk

3 eggs

1 teaspoon coconut extract

CREAM CHEESE ICING

1 (8-ounce) package cream cheese, softened

1/2 cup (1 stick) margarine, softened

1 teaspoon vanilla extract

5 1/2 cups sifted confectioners' sugar

3 cups sweetened flaked coconut for decorating

Serves 12

- *For the cake,* butter and flour two 8-inch round cake pans.
- Combine the cake mix, coconut milk, eggs and coconut extract in a large mixing bowl. Beat for 2 minutes or until smooth. Pour the mixture into the prepared cake pans.
- Bake at 350 degrees for 30 to 35 minutes or until a toothpick inserted in the center comes out clean.
- Remove from the oven and cool in the pans on a wire rack for 15 minutes. Remove the cakes from the pans and cool completely on a wire rack. Chill, covered, in the refrigerator. It is much easier and less crumbly to ice a cold cake.
- *For the icing,* beat the cream cheese and margarine in a mixing bowl until light and fluffy. Add the vanilla and mix well. Add in the confectioners' sugar gradually, beating well after each addition. This makes enough to frost the top and side of an 8 to 9-inch layered cake. It can be stored in the refrigerator for 2 weeks. Bring to room temperature before frosting the cakes.
- *To assemble,* ice both layers of the cake and cover with the coconut flakes. Place 1 iced cake layer on a serving plate and stack the other layer on top. Smooth the entire surface with icing and coconut flakes. Refrigerate the cake if needed. Bring the cake to room temperature before serving.

thai tidbit

You must remove your shoes before entering a
Thai house or temple.

I have served this tart for so many years that it has become my signature dessert after a Thai meal. It's cool and creamy, bursting with lime flavor, and served in a crunchy crust. It's a great way to introduce tropical fruits to your friends. I use a combination of seasonal fruits. If you can't find one kind, just add another. We want different flavors and colors together here. Experimenting with different fruits is a lot of fun!

Lime Curd Tart with Tropical Fruits

CRUST

2/3 cup sliced almonds

1/4 cup sugar

1/4 teaspoon salt

1 cup vanilla wafer crumbs

1/4 cup unsalted butter, melted

LIME CURD

1 cup plus 2 tablespoons sugar

1/2 cup (1 stick) unsalted butter, cut into pieces

4 eggs, lightly beaten

2 egg yolks, lightly beaten

1/2 cup fresh lime juice

1 tablespoon freshly grated lime zest (from about 2 limes)

FRESH FRUITS

1 1/2 cups diced pineapple

1 cup diced mangoes

1 cup diced kiwifruit

1 cup red raspberries

1 cup thinly sliced star fruit for garnish

Mint for garnish

Serves 8

- *For the crust,* spread the almonds in a single layer on a baking sheet. Bake at 375 degrees for 5 to 8 minutes or until light brown. Let the almonds cool completely. Grind the almonds in a food processor until fine.
- Coat a 9-inch tart pan with removable bottom with nonstick cooking spray.
- Combine the almonds, sugar, salt, vanilla wafer crumbs and butter in a small bowl and mix well.
- Sprinkle the almond mixture into the pan and press the mixture firmly over the bottom and up the side of the pan.
- Bake at 350 degrees for 10 minutes or until golden brown. Remove to a wire rack to cool completely.
- *For the lime curd,* combine the sugar, butter, eggs, egg yolks and lime juice in a saucepan and mix well.
- Cook over low heat for 10 to 12 minutes, or until the mixture is thick enough to coat the back of a spoon, stirring continuously.
- Strain the mixture through a fine-mesh sieve into a bowl. Stir in the lime zest and let cool.
- Cover with plastic wrap, pressing the plastic wrap to the surface of the lime curd, and refrigerate. This can be made up to one week in advance and stored in the refrigerator.
- *To assemble,* spread the lime curd evenly into the crust. Chill the tart for 1 to 12 hours. Longer storage will make the crust soggy.
- *To serve,* remove the side of the tart pan. Slice the tart into 8 pieces and place 1 slice on each dessert plate. Scatter the fruits over the tart slices. Garnish each slice with star fruit and a sprig of mint.

Once I was hired to make bite-size goodies for wedding guests to take home. The reception theme was tropical, so I made lime bars and added coconut to achieve the exotic goal. It turned out to be a rich, moist dessert with an explosion of lime flavor.

Key Lime Coconut Bars

COCONUT BUTTER CRUST

1³/4 cups all-purpose flour

1/4 cup confectioners' sugar

1/4 teaspoon salt

1¹/2 cups flaked coconut

³/4 cup (1¹/2 sticks) plus 2 tablespoons unsalted butter, cut into pieces

1 egg

1 teaspoon vanilla extract

LIME FILLING

6 eggs

3 cups sugar

1 tablespoon freshly grated lime zest (from about 2 limes)

1 cup plus 2 tablespoons lime juice

1 teaspoon baking powder

1/2 cup all-purpose flour

Confectioners' sugar for dusting

Makes 24 bars

- *For the crust,* place the flour, sugar, salt and flaked coconut in a food processor and pulse to combine. Add the butter and process until coarse crumbs form. Add the egg and vanilla and process until the mixture forms a ball.
- Press the dough into a 9×13-inch baking pan and bake at 350 degrees for 15 minutes or until light brown. Remove to a wire rack to cool completely.
- *For the lime filling,* combine the eggs, sugar, lime zest and lime juice in a mixing bowl. Beat on low speed for 2 minutes or until smooth. Add the baking powder and flour and continue beating on low speed until well blended. Pour the filling over the crust.
- Bake at 350 degrees for 35 minutes or until the filling is set. Remove to a wire rack to cool completely.
- Dust generously with confectioners' sugar and cut into 1¹/2- to 2-inch squares.
- Refrigerate any leftovers.

garnishing ideas & techniques

In the Kingdom of Thailand food is always presented with the utmost care and beauty. My mom always placed pretty garnishes on the serving dishes for us to look at, and I do the same thing for my children and guests. These are Thai-style garnishes I learned growing up. This will take a little time, effort, and practice for you to achieve, but you will soon impress your family and friends with these garnishes.

There are other simple ways to garnish without a lot of knife usage. Use uniquely shaped dishes or take advantage of color. Don't overdo it. My favorite everyday easy garnish is a tomato rose. It's simple, but beautiful. I hope you will be inspired to learn these techniques.

cucumber leaf

Wash a cucumber and lay it on a cutting board. Cut it in half vertically. Turn the cucumber up, with the cut bottom serving as a base. Make three diagonal cuts around the cucumber, starting at the tip and proceeding to the base. Discard the core. Trim the three pieces into the rough outline of a leaf. Next, make three or four small V-cuts on each side of the leaf to make the leaf pointed.

The following steps require making indentations in the cucumber to highlight the center vein and leaflets. Do not cut all the way through the cucumber to make these indentations. In essence, you are only removing the skin. To make the center vein, cut a $1/16$-inch indentation on both sides of the center of the leaf, leaving a $1/16$-inch strip of skin as the vein. Next, trace an approximate $1/8$-inch border around each leaflet. Peel away the center skin of each leaflet to the vein. The leaf can be made several hours ahead; wrap in a wet paper towel and store in the refrigerator until ready to use.

chili flower

Use a long slender pepper like cayenne. Wear rubber gloves to prevent burning. Lay the pepper flat on a cutting board. Using a small paring knife, make four or five slits from the pointed tip to about $1/4$ inch from the stem; cut all the way through and all the way around. Place in a bowl of ice water and store in the refrigerator overnight or for up to three days.

green onion curls

Trim the roots off a green onion. Cut the onion into $2^{1}/_{2}$-inch pieces. Use a small paring knife to make repeated $1/2$-inch incisions on each end of the piece. The white part of the onion will require more incisions. Place the pieces in a bowl of ice water overnight in the refrigerator. The longer it sits the curlier it will be.

radish mushroom

Turn a radish root side up. Visualize the stem of the mushroom and make two cuts halfway down. Cut horizontally from the outside of the radish toward the middle to meet the first two cuts. The result will be the rough shape of a mushroom. Trim the exterior of the rough stem by making the same first two cuts but rotated ninety degrees. This will give you a square stem; go ahead and cut the angles of the stem to make it round. Turn the mushroom upright. Use a paring knife to randomly peel portions of the cap off to make small circles. Place in a bowl of ice water and store in the refrigerator for up to three days.

radish flower I

Hold a radish upright. Make two V-cuts in the top of the radish $1/3$ of the way through. The cuts should be equally placed so that they form a plus sign. Make two additional V-cuts in the center of the first two cuts. The result will be eight sections, which will become eight petals. Carefully peel down the skin from the cuts. Make sure not to peel away the bottom $1/4$-inch of the petal. Place in a bowl of ice water and store in the refrigerator for up to three days. The longer it sits the wider the petals will open.

radish flower II

You will need a carving tool for this flower. Using your carving tool, gently carve a long strip downward, leaving it intact. Repeat the same procedure to finish the first layer and for all the inner layers. It should look like a chrysanthemum. Place in a bowl of ice water and store in the refrigerator.

tomato rose I

I use a Roma tomato for this one. You're welcome to use the large beefsteak tomato, which will produce a larger rose. Turn the tomato upside down. Using a small paring knife, gently peel the skin around the tomato, trying not to cut into the flesh. Peel until all the skin is off. The goal is to have one strip of skin. If you have two strips you can still assemble it into a rose but more than two strips will require you to start over. Loosely roll the skin, starting from the bottom of the tomato. Eventually you will have a rose in your hand. This rose can be made several hours ahead; wrap in a wet paper towel and store in the refrigerator until ready to use.

tomato rose II

Cut a large tomato in half. One half makes one rose. Lay one half flat on a cutting board and slice it thinly. Start with the smallest slice as the center bud. In ascending order, wrap the remaining slices around the bud. Some of the slices will overlap. Use a spatula to transfer the garnishing rose to a serving plate. This rose can only be made right before serving; it cannot be stored because the juice will run out.

1 whole fresh coconut

2 star fruit (carambola)

3 plantain

4 coconut half

5 whole shallots, sliced

6 fresh ginger

7 fresh galangal

8 Japaneese eggplant

9 pickled garlic

10 whole garlic

11 green papaya half

12 grated papaya

13 pickled mustard cabbage

14 canned straw mushrooms

15 cayenne peppers

16 fresh Kaffir lime leaves

17 lemongrass, sliced and whole

18 sliced lime

dry ingredients

1 dried egg noodles

2 dried tamarind pulp

3 grated dried radish

4 shrimp paste

5 dried shrimp

6 palm sugar

7 spring roll wrapper

8 fresh rice noodles (broad)

9 dried rice sticks

10 round and square
    won ton wrappers

11 turmeric powder

12 coriander powder

13 curry powder

14 dried salted plums

15 dried chili peppers

16 dried galangal

17 dried egg noodles (small)

18 dried thin rice noodles

19 glass noodles

20 fish sauce

21 red chili dipping sauce

22 coconut milk

23 roasted red chili paste

24 green curry paste

25 red curry paste

26 spicy Thai chili sauce (sriracha)

27 soy sauce

28 light soy sauce

29 black soy sauce

30 sweet soy sauce

31 oyster sauce

For more information on
Thai Kitchen's products, call
1-800-967-THAI or 1-510-675-9025
or go online to www.thaikitchen.com

glossary

Bamboo Shoots (naw-mai-pai)

For the Green Chicken Curry recipe in this cookbook, use already sliced bamboo shoots in a can (16 or 20 ounces). Drain and it's ready to be used. It's quite mild, bordering on tasteless, but it adds crunch to the dish.

Basil, Thai/Holy Basil (bai-ho-ra-pah/bai-gra-pao)

For curry recipes that call for basil, we typically use Thai basil. It has longer and more slender leaves and darker purple stems than sweet basil. It also provides a warmer flavor. If Thai basil is not available, sweet basil is a good substitute. However, when the recipe calls for holy basil, there is no substitute.

Holy basil has thick and somewhat curly leaves, with a lot of heat. If fresh is not available, you can purchase it in a jar with the sauce already made. It's easy to grow your own holy basil; you can order the plant from Logee's Greenhouse (www.logees.com or call 1-888-330-8038).

Chili Paste, Roasted (naam-prik-pao)

This paste is made from a mixture of shrimp paste, garlic, onion, chili peppers, and other flavorings. It's used for spicy/sour soups, chicken and cashew, and even Thai coconut chicken soup. It's really not spicy like curry paste and it has already been cooked. Thais use it as a dip for shrimp chips or mix it with rice. It comes in a glass jar; store in the refrigerator after opening. The Thai Kitchen brand is called Roasted Red Chili Paste.

Chili Peppers (prik)

When recipes in this book call for chili peppers, you can use a variety of peppers, including serrano, cayenne, Tabasco, and of course, Thai chili peppers. The shape in this case doesn't matter, since all you need is the heat.

Chili Sauce, Sweet (naam-jim-gai)

This sweet-and-sour sauce is used as a dip for grilled chicken of any type, not just Esaan style. It's also good for grilled pork and grilled beef. It is more sweet than spicy. The Thai Kitchen brand is called Red Chili Dipping Sauce.

Cilantro, or Chinese Parsley (pak-chee)

You won't have any trouble finding this aromatic herb. It's sold at any grocery store. It is used in a number of Thai salads and as a garnish in soups and other dishes.

Cilantro Root (raak-pak-chee)

In Thai recipes cilantro roots are used in meat-marinating mixtures. It has a very intense coriander-like flavor. In fact, coriander is the seed of this plant and can be used as a substitute. Sadly, in the United States the roots are typically cut before arriving in the grocery store, so your best option is to grow your own. To substitute, $1/2$ teaspoon of coriander equals one cilantro root.

Coconut (ma-prao)

The coconuts sold in American grocery stores are really just the inner shell; the outside shell has already been removed. Coconuts are sold at different ages. Younger coconuts are lighter in color and are used primarily for sweets, especially the grated flesh. The darker ones are used to make coconut milk.

The clear juice inside the coconut is used as a drink; it is not coconut milk. In this book, the main coconut ingredient is the milk. For coconut cake I use dried flakes from a gourmet baking store, but sweetened dried flakes are fine.

Coconut Milk (ga-ti)

In Thailand we wouldn't think of using canned coconut milk because fresh milk is readily available. However, canned coconut milk is usually the easiest option and it works quite well. True, the fragrance of fresh milk is absent, but the convenience and storage life compensate well for this deficiency. Shake the can well before opening. If it is solidified, stir well before using. An opened can needs to be used within two or three days.

To make fresh coconut milk, hold a coconut in your palm over a sink. Hit the circumference of the shell a few times with a hammer. It should crack in half on its own. A bad coconut will require several hits before cracking (about five minutes of hitting). Grate the white interior of the coconut with a small handheld grater, which looks like a large zester. Or hit the coconut halves into smaller pieces, detach the brown shell from the white flesh, and place the flesh in a food processor. Put grated coconut flesh in a medium-size bowl. Add one cup of water and squeeze the mixture between the palms of your hands for a few minutes or until you see the white liquid.

Strain through a sieve into another bowl. Repeat the process of adding water and squeezing until the water is almost clear. Discard the flesh and use the milk immediately or store in a refrigerator for up to two days. The milk can also be frozen. One coconut should yield approximately three cups of milk.

Coriander (met-pahk-chee)

These small round seeds come from cilantro, or the Chinese parsley plant. Coriander has a mild aroma and warm flavor. Thais normally use whole seeds in Mussaman and Panang curries. The powdered one I use here gives extra flavor as a substitute for cilantro root, which we use widely in Thailand, but which is not available in the United States.

Curry Pastes (kruang-gaeng)

The imported Thai brands come in two forms: the Mae-Sri or Mae Ploy brands are in four-ounce cans, while the spicier Thai Kitchen brand comes in a jar, so you can refrigerate the unused portions. If you feel adventurous, you can make your paste from scratch using the recipes on pages 87, 88, and 89.

Curry Powder (pohng-ga-ree)

A mixture of different aromatic spices, the Madras style produces the most intense flavors and aromas. You can find it in an Indian or oriental grocery store. Curry paste, not curry powder, is the key ingredient in Thai curries. Curry powder is used to enhance the flavor of certain curries, such as yellow chicken curry or Burmese curry.

Fish Sauce (naam-pblah)

A fermented anchovy extract, this salting agent is the secret of Thai cooking. There are many brands available and each has a different level of sodium. Thai Kitchen fish sauce is a good-quality sauce. Experiment with a small amount before using. It has a very strong, intimidating smell to it. It's normally stored at room temperature, but if it is not used often, I'd advise storing it in the refrigerator.

Galangal (kah)

This funny looking long-legged rhizome is related to the ginger family but the taste is different. It is an essential ingredient for curry paste and is the core ingredient in dtom-ka-gai. In soups it is sliced into round disks and in curry pastes it is ground. It's too chewy to eat but is used for the flavoring. Use a fresh root if you can and freeze the unused portion. If worst comes to worst, you can use dry galangal, already sliced. It tastes okay and there is no need to soak; just rinse.

Galangal Powder (pohng-kah)

If you are unable to find fresh galangal, then you must add this powder to Thai coconut chicken soup. However, the dry powder does not have nearly the flavor of fresh galangal.

Kaffir Lime Leaf (and whole) (bai-ma-grood)

This lime is similar in size to regular limes but looks quite different. It has a bumpy, knobby skin with a stronger fragrance. Its zest is essential for Thai curry pastes. The juice is far too sour to be eaten but can be used for washing and cleaning products. The leaves look like a slender number eight: small on top, large on the bottom, and a vein in the middle.

It is used mainly in soups and curries but also in certain kinds of salads. In soups it is best to use small whole leaves but bigger leaves can be used if torn in half. In curries the leaves are stacked together and rolled like a cigarette; trim the stem (if any) and cut the stack as finely as possible. The leaves freeze wonderfully in a freezer-proof bag. Rinse with hot water to thaw. It is quite easy to grow your own plant. Logee's greenhouse sells a great-quality Kaffir plant: it comes in 4-inch and 6-inch pots. I highly recommend purchasing the plant if you plan to use a lot of it.

Lemongrass (dtah-krai)

This tall grassy-like herb has a pronounced citrus scent. It is essential for Thai cooking and is used in a variety of dishes, from curry pastes, to soups, to seafood. It's sold in a bundle of four or five stems tied with a rubber band. Thais use only the stalks in cooking; we discard the leaves. To get the most flavor, crush or pound the bottom (the biggest part of the plant) with a meat mallet or pestle. Cut into 2-inch-long strips and use in soups. For curry pastes, it is cut vertically into fine slices.

I don't think there is a real substitute for lemongrass. Some say you may substitute lemon zest but to me it doesn't taste the same. It has become more available in the United States. You can also grow your own if you wish. I live in Kansas and it does not survive the winter, so bring the plant indoors. The stalks can be stored in a freezer for up to three months.

Limes (ma-nao)

There are two kinds of limes available in most grocery stores: the small Florida Key limes and Persian limes. You can use them interchangeably. Key limes have a more intense lime fragrance but it takes less time to squeeze the larger Persian limes. I look for plump limes with a shiny smooth skin. The thinner the skin the more juice there is.

Mustard Cabbage, Pickled (pak-gaad-dong)

This salty and sour pickled cabbage is eaten as a condiment with Chiang Mai noodles and Green Chicken Curry. It is sold in a plastic bag. After opening, store in the refrigerator for up to one week.

Noodles, Dried Egg (bah-me)

Made from wheat flour and eggs, these noodles are used in Chiang Mai noodles and other dishes. It comes in different sizes and shapes. I most frequently use a package with several small rounds of compressed noodles. The serving size is typically one round per person.

Noodles, Glass or Cellophane Noodles (woon-sen)

Made from ground mung bean flour (bean sprouts grow from mung beans), it's hard and opaque but when cooked it becomes translucent. It comes in a package of several bundles. Soak in water for fifteen minutes to reconstitute the shape; then drain and use it according to the recipe. I use glass noodles in spring rolls and glass noodle salad. It can also be used in stir-fried dishes due to its soft, slippery texture.

Noodles, Rice or Rice Sticks (gway-tio)

These come in multiple sizes. They are made of ground rice and water, rolled out like pasta, and cut into different sizes. In the United States I prefer to use dried noodles because of the longer shelf life. The fresh noodles become brittle and hard to work with. However, pad-si-ew requires fresh noodles. The dried noodles can be stored for many months. Soak in hot water for fifteen minutes and drain before using. Thai Kitchen offers thin rice noodles and Pad Thai noodles.

Oyster Sauce (sautd-hoi-nang-rom)

Another salting agent, this is a thick brown liquid with oyster extract. It thickens a sauce as it seasons. All soy sauces and oyster sauces are used for stir-fried dishes and noodles. They are never used in curries or salads.

Palm Sugar (naam-thaan-bpuk)

It should be called coconut sugar since it's made from the sap of coconut trees. The sap is slowly cooked until it becomes thick and light brown. Once cooked it is poured into round molds. In the United States it is sold in either a package of round disks or in a plastic jar; I prefer the round disks as they are convenient for measuring. Store in an airtight container at room temperature, but beware of ants.

Papaya, Green (ma-la-gaw)

A green papaya is an unripe papaya. When green, it is used as a vegetable and is bland and crunchy. However, when combined with the intense ingredients found in a papaya salad, the taste is anything but bland. Pick a firm papaya with no blemishes. It can be kept in the refrigerator for up to two weeks.

Pepper, White (prik-thai)

In Thailand we use this milder pepper to season, but black pepper is also acceptable. Actually, white pepper is really black pepper without skin. Either one works well and will not change the flavor. I like to grind my own peppercorns. You can find ground white pepper, but I find it to be too powdery.

Plum, Salted (buoy-kem)

This ingredient is used in the making of plum sauce for spring rolls. This salty and sour dried whitish brown plum is sold in a small plastic container. Discard the seed after using. You can purchase already-made plum sauce but I find its plum flavor too pronounced.

Radish, Sweetened, Salted, Dried (sometimes mislabeled "turnip") (hua-pak-gaad)

This daikon radish is white when fresh but becomes shriveled and brown when preserved. It sounds confusing to be sweetened and salted at the same time. The salt is used for preserving, while sugar is used for flavoring. If you can find only the salted kind, it is okay to use. I prefer the shredded kind, which is sold in 8-ounce packages, as it takes less time to chop. In this book it's called for in the Pad Thai recipe.

Rice Flour (bpang-kao-gao)

Made from finely ground and pulverized rice, it's light and airy and used as a coating for fried dishes. It's also used sometimes as a thickening agent. It comes in a small plastic bag and can be stored in a freezer-proof bag for up to six months.

Rice, Sticky or glutinous rice (kao-nee-o)

It contains a high starch content, making it sticky enough to eat by hand. It is eaten with Esaan-style food and is used in desserts such as sticky rice and mangoes. It needs to be soaked at least two hours or overnight and then steamed. A little bit goes a long way; it's a lot heavier than regular rice.

Rice, Thai Jasmine (kao-hohm-mah-li)

Of course, I only use rice from Thailand. Jasmine rice produces a fluffy, aromatic, and tender grain. It comes in different sizes ranging from five pounds to fifty pounds. Rice can be stored in freezer-proof bags for longer storage.

Shrimp, Dried (gung-haeng)

This salted pale red preserved shrimp is used primarily in papaya salad and Pad Thai. Use a larger size shrimp as the smaller ones seem to have too much red dye added. Store in a freezer-proof bag for up to six months. Thaw in hot water, drain, and use. It can also be kept in the refrigerator for short-term storage. I rinse the shrimp before using to get rid of the extra salt and occasional debris.

Shrimp Paste (ga-bpi)

This is an indispensable ingredient to curry paste. It's purplish gray with a strong shrimp odor and salty flavor. It gives the curry the ability to adhere to other ingredients. It's also used in spicy Thai vegetable dip and roasted chili paste. It comes in a small plastic container. Keep in the refrigerator, though in Thailand it's kept at room temperature but it is used very frequently. If you buy already-made curry paste, there is no need to buy shrimp paste at all. To use, put a small amount in foil (my mom uses a banana leaf) and roast for five minutes at high heat. I recommend that you do this on an outdoor grill due to the intolerable fumes.

Soy Sauce (sautd)

A sauce made of soy beans, the Thai brands are less salty than brands from other countries.

Soy Sauce, Black/Sweet Soy Sauce (see-ew-dum/see-ew-wan)

These two sauces look identical. They look like thick molasses with the aroma of soy sauce. Use sparingly in some dishes. The black soy sauce has more saltiness while the sweet soy sauce is used as its name implies.

Soy Sauce, Light (see-ew-kao)

Don't confuse it with low-sodium soy sauce. In Thai it translates as "white soy sauce." It's a milder soy sauce. There are a couple of variants, including one with mushroom extract. It is good for marinating meat.

Spices, Miscellaneous (kruang-thet)

Cinnamon, nutmeg, star anise, and cardamom are used to make Panang curry paste, while caraway seeds are used to make Mussaman curry paste. Thai cooking uses more herbs than spices. Spices are limited to curry dishes.

Spring Roll Wrappers (bpang-bpaw-bpia)

There is no egg in these wrappers, making them light and crispy. Typically found in the frozen section of an oriental grocery store, they are not to be confused with Vietnamese dried rice paper. Fresh spring roll wrappers are available in Thailand and are used for fresh spring rolls. Summer wrapped rolls need to be credited to Vietnamese cuisine, not Thai.

Sriracha Sauce (sautd-sriracha)

A spicy chili sauce used as a dip for fried food, grilled food, and even omelets. It's the most versatile sauce when you want an extra zing. It takes its name from a region in eastern Thailand. The Thai Kitchen brand is called Spicy Thai Chili Sauce.

Tamarind (mah-cahm-bpiahk)

The tamarind tree produces a green pod that turns brown when ripe. The brown pod is what we use in cooking. It has a dry sticky brown pulp with black seeds inside, though we don't use the seeds. The pulp gives an intense sourness to food. If tamarind is not available, you can substitute lime juice. You can buy the seeded pulp in a rectangular block; break off pieces as needed.

To make tamarind juice, soak one piece in hot water in a ratio of one part tamarind to three parts water until softened, about five minutes. Strain the pulp and use the juice. It's safe to store at room temperature and it has an indefinite shelf life, though I store mine in a container in the refrigerator.

Turmeric Powder (pohng-ka-min)

This small root (a rhizome), about the size of a finger, has a deep golden color. When peeled, the color is almost orange. It's readily available in Thailand, so Thais use fresh turmeric, which produces a superior aroma and color. In the United States, we use it in powdered form. It is used in satay and some southern curries.

Won Ton Wrapper (tee-hah-kanom-jeeb)

Made from wheat flour dough and eggs, it's used for Chinese dumplings. In this book it's used for Steamed Pork Dumplings in the Street Snack chapter. You can find it fresh or frozen and it comes in either small rounds or squares. Freeze the unused portions.

index

Accompaniments. *See also* Sauces, Dipping
    Cucumber Relish, 15
    Spicy Red Sauce, 39

Appetizers. *See also* Sauces, Dipping
    Corn Cakes with Spicy Cucumber Sauce, 55
    Curry Puffs, 92
    Dried Thai Beef, 93
    Fish Cakes, 22
    Fried Tofu, 54
    Fried Won Tons, 94
    Pork Satay, 14
    Shrimp Toast, 93
    Spring Rolls with Pork Filling, 12
    Steamed Pork Dumplings, 95

Banana
    Fried Bananas, 96
    White Chocolate Shortcakes with
        Caramelized Bananas, 102

Beans. *See also* Bean Sprouts
    Fish Cakes, 22
    Papaya Salad, 31
    Spicy Ground Beef with Green Beans, 63

Bean Sprouts
    Fried Mussels Pancake with Bean Sprouts, 50
    Pad Thai, 16

Beef
    Beef and Mushrooms in Oyster Sauce, 46
    Beef Panang Curry, 24
    Beef with Bell Peppers, 47
    Chiang Mai Noodles in Curry Sauce, 71
    Dried Thai Beef, 93
    Ginger Beef, 82

    Grilled Beef Salad, 76
    Grilled Pork or Beef, 32
    Mussamun Beef Curry, 62
    Northeastern (Esaan) Beef Salad, 33
    Spicy Ground Beef with Green Beans, 63

Beverages
    Iced Coffee, 97
    Limeade, 26
    Watermelon Smoothie, 19

Catfish
    Fish Cakes, 22
    Puffed-Crispy Fried Catfish Salad, 40

Chicken
    Chicken and Cashews, 25
    Chicken Fried Rice, 49
    Coconut Chicken Soup with
        Galangal, 23
    Curry Puffs, 92
    Dad's Burmese Curry, 65
    Green Chicken Curry, 64
    Grilled Chicken, 34
    Northeastern Chicken Salad, 34
    Stir-Fried Broad Noodles with Garlicky
        Chicken and Collard Greens, 72
    Stir-Fried Noodles with Chicken and
        Mixed Vegetable Sauce, 73
    Yellow Chicken Curry, 63

Chocolate
    White Chocolate Crème Brûlée, 103
    White Chocolate Raspberry
        Cheesecake, 100
    White Chocolate Shortcakes with
        Caramelized Bananas, 102

index

Coconut
Chiang Mai Noodles in Curry Sauce, 71
Coconut Cake with Cream Cheese Icing, 104
Coconut Chicken Soup with Galangal, 23
Coconut Flan, 35
Coconut Ice Cream, 18
Fried Bananas, 96
Fried Ice Cream Balls with Caramel
   Sauce, 66
Green Chicken Curry, 64
Green Curry with Mushrooms, 57
Key Lime Coconut Bars, 106
Mussamun Beef Curry, 62
Yellow Chicken Curry, 63

Collard Greens
Stir-Fried Broad Noodles with Garlicky
   Chicken and Collard Greens, 72
Stir-Fried Mixed Vegetables, 56

Corn
Corn Cakes with Spicy Cucumber Sauce, 55
Stir-Fried Mixed Vegetables, 56

Cucumbers
Cucumber Relish, 15
Glass Noodle Soup, 78
Grilled Beef Salad, 76
Spicy Cucumber Sauce, 55
Tangy Cucumber Sauce, 22

Curry. *See also* Curry Paste
Beef Panang Curry, 24
Dad's Burmese Curry, 65
Green Chicken Curry, 64
Green Curry with Mushrooms, 57
Mussamun Beef Curry, 62

Spicy Ground Beef with Green Beans, 63
Yellow Chicken Curry, 63

Curry Paste
Chiang Mai Noodles in Curry Sauce, 71
Dad's Burmese Curry, 65
Green Curry Paste, 89
Mussamun Curry Paste, 89
Panang Curry Paste, 87
Red Curry Paste, 87
Yellow Curry Paste, 88

Desserts. *See also* Ice Cream; Pies/Tarts;
   Sauces, Dessert
Coconut Cake with Cream Cheese Icing, 104
Coconut Flan, 35
Fried Bananas, 96
Key Lime Coconut Bars, 106
Pineapple Napoleons, 59
Sticky Rice and Mangoes, 27
White Chocolate Crème Brûlée, 103
White Chocolate Raspberry
   Cheesecake, 100
White Chocolate Shortcakes with
   Caramelized Bananas, 102

Egg Dishes
Omelet with Pork, 85
Savory Herbed Custard, 79
Stuffed Omelet, 84

Eggplant
Green Chicken Curry, 64
Green Curry with Mushrooms, 57
Grilled Eggplant Salad, 58

Fish. *See* Catfish; Red Snapper

index

Fruit. *See also* Banana; Kiwifruit; Lime; Mango;
    Papaya; Pineapple; Raspberry; Star Fruit
    Blueberry Ice Cream Pie, 43
    Fresh Fruit Platter, 79
    Watermelon Smoothie, 19

Glass Noodles
    Glass Noodle Salad, 26
    Glass Noodle Soup, 78
    Spring Rolls with Pork Filling, 12

Ice Cream
    Blueberry Ice Cream Pie, 43
    Coconut Ice Cream, 18
    Fried Ice Cream Balls with Caramel
        Sauce, 66

Kiwifruit
    Fresh Fruit Platter, 79
    Lime Curd Tart with Tropical Fruits, 105

Lemongrass
    Coconut Chicken Soup with
        Galangal, 23
    Red Curry Paste, 87
    Spicy Shrimp Soup, 38

Lime
    Key Lime Coconut Bars, 106
    Limeade, 26
    Lime Curd Tart with Tropical Fruits, 105

Mango
    Fresh Fruit Platter, 79
    Lime Curd Tart with Tropical Fruits, 105
    Puffed-Crispy Fried Catfish Salad, 40
    Sticky Rice and Mangoes, 27

Mushrooms
    Beef and Mushrooms in Oyster Sauce, 46
    Coconut Chicken Soup with Galangal, 23
    Green Curry with Mushrooms, 57
    Spicy Shrimp Soup, 38

Noodles. *See also* Glass Noodles;
    Rice Noodles
    Chiang Mai Noodles in Curry Sauce, 71

Papaya
    Fresh Fruit Platter, 79
    Papaya Salad, 31

Peppers
    Beef Panang Curry, 24
    Beef with Bell Peppers, 47
    Dipping Sauce, 54
    Ginger Beef, 82
    Green Chicken Curry, 64
    Green Curry Paste, 89
    Green Curry with Mushrooms, 57
    Grilled Eggplant Salad, 58
    Papaya Salad, 31
    Pork with Holy Basil, 48
    Red Curry Paste, 87
    Seafood Dipping Sauce, 42
    Spicy Red Sauce, 39
    Stir-Fried Mixed Vegetables, 56

Pies/Tarts
    Blueberry Ice Cream Pie, 43
    Lime Curd Tart with Tropical Fruits, 105

Pineapple
    Fresh Fruit Platter, 79
    Lime Curd Tart with Tropical Fruits, 105

Mussamun Beef Curry, 62
Pineapple Napoleons, 59

Pork
Fried Won Tons, 94
Garlic Pepper Pork, 83
Glass Noodle Salad, 26
Glass Noodle Soup, 78
Grilled Pork or Beef, 32
Omelet with Pork, 85
Pad Thai, 16
Pork Satay, 14
Pork with Holy Basil, 48
Spring Rolls with Pork Filling, 12
Steamed Pork Dumplings, 95
Stuffed Omelet, 84

Potatoes
Curry Puffs, 92
Mussamun Beef Curry, 62
Yellow Chicken Curry, 63

Raspberry
Lime Curd Tart with Tropical Fruits, 105
Raspberry Sauce, 101
White Chocolate Raspberry
    Cheesecake, 100

Red Snapper
Red Snapper Steamed in
    Lime Juice, 77
Red Snapper with Spicy Red Sauce, 39

Rice. *See also* Sticky Rice
Chicken Fried Rice, 49
Crab Fried Rice, 41
Tips on Cooking Rice, 51

Rice Noodles
Crispy Noodles, 70
Pad Thai, 16
Stir-Fried Broad Noodles with Garlicky
    Chicken and Collard Greens, 72
Stir-Fried Noodles with Chicken and
    Mixed Vegetable Sauce, 73

Salads
Glass Noodle Salad, 26
Grilled Beef Salad, 76
Grilled Eggplant Salad, 58
Northeastern Chicken Salad, 34
Northeastern (Esaan) Beef
    Salad, 33
Papaya Salad, 31
Puffed-Crispy Fried Catfish
    Salad, 40

Sauces, Dessert
Blueberry Sauce, 43
Caramel Sauce, 67
Pineapple Sauce, 59
Raspberry Sauce, 101

Sauces, Dipping
Dipping Sauce, 54
Fish Sauce with Chili
    Peppers, 86
Satay Sauce, 15
Sauce for Boiled Eggs, 86
Seafood Dipping Sauce, 42
Soy Dipping Sauce, 95
Spicy Cucumber Sauce, 55
Spicy Dipping Sauce, 32
Spring Roll Sauce, 13
Tangy Cucumber Sauce, 22

index

Seafood. *See also* Shrimp
    Crab Fried Rice, 41
    Fried Mussels Pancake with
        Bean Sprouts, 50
    Grilled Mixed Seafood, 42

Shrimp
    Crispy Noodles, 70
    Glass Noodle Salad, 26
    Pad Thai, 16
    Papaya Salad, 31
    Shrimp Toast, 93
    Spicy Shrimp Soup, 38

Simple Syrup, 19

Soups
    Coconut Chicken Soup with Galangal, 23
    Glass Noodle Soup, 78
    Spicy Shrimp Soup, 38

Star Fruit
    Fresh Fruit Platter, 79
    Lime Curd Tart with Tropical Fruits, 105

Sticky Rice
    Rice Powder, 30
    Sticky Rice, 30
    Sticky Rice and Mangoes, 27

Stir Fry
    Beef and Mushrooms in Oyster Sauce, 46
    Beef with Bell Peppers, 47
    Chicken and Cashews, 25
    Chicken and Fried Rice, 49

Crab Fried Rice, 41
Fried Mussels Pancake with
    Bean Sprouts, 50
Garlic Pepper Pork, 83
Ginger Beef, 82
Pad Thai, 16
Pork with Holy Basil, 48
Stir-Fried Broad Noodles with Garlicky
    Chicken and Collard Greens, 72
Stir-Fried Mixed Vegetables, 56
Stir-Fried Noodles with Chicken and Mixed
    Vegetable Sauce, 73

Thai Stock
    Glass Noodle Soup, 78
    Stir-Fried Noodles with Chicken and Mixed
        Vegetable Sauce, 73
    Thai Stock, 85

Tofu
    Fried Tofu, 54
    Glass Noodle Soup, 78

Tomatoes
    Chicken Fried Rice, 49
    Dad's Burmese Curry, 65
    Grilled Beef Salad, 76
    Papaya Salad, 31

Vegetables. *See also* Beans; Collard Greens;
    Corn; Cucumbers; Eggplant;
    Mushrooms; Peppers; Potatoes;
    Tomatoes
    Stir-Fried Noodles with Chicken and Mixed
        Vegetable Sauce, 73

lemongrass & limes

Thai Flavors with Naam Pruitt

P.O. Box 1243

Independence, Kansas 67301

620-331-4055

Name _____

Street Address _____

City _____ State _____ Zip _____

Telephone _____

Please send _____ copies of *lemongrass & limes* at $26.50 each $ _____

Kansas residents add 7.6% sales tax $ _____

Postage and handling at $4.95 each $ _____

Total $ _____

Method of Payment: [   ] MasterCard   [   ] VISA

[   ] Check enclosed payable to Naam Pruitt

Account Number _____ Expiration Date _____

Signature _____

Additional copies may also be ordered online at *www.lemongrassandlimes.com*.

Photocopies will be accepted.

Critics are raving about *Lemongrass & Limes: Thai Flavors with Naam Pruitt*. You will, too, after trying the delicious, and surprisingly simple, recipes in this book. Read on to hear what the author's biggest fans have to say.

"She's the best cook and the best mama in the world!"
Anna Pruitt, author's daughter

"Well, I love her cooking just as much as I love her."
Bennett Pruitt, author's son

"What's for supper?"
Dennis Pruitt, author's husband

"Woof! Woof!"
Champ, author's dog